Under His Divine Gaze

A SPIRITUAL MEMOIR

MONIQUE PILON-FRASCHETTI

One Printers Way
Altona, MB R0G 0B0
Canada

www.friesenpress.com

ISBN
978-1-03-914149-0 (Hardcover)
978-1-03-914148-3 (Paperback)
978-1-03-914150-6 (eBook)

1. Religion, Christian Life, Spiritual Growth.

Distributed to the trade by The Ingram Book Company

For
Those whom I cherish on Earth and in Heaven
and to
those who believe in sacred, everlasting love

Table of Contents

Acknowledgements

To my guardian angel, who lovingly and diligently safeguards me all the days of my life. Your aid is inestimable. My heart abounds with thankfulness.

To my caring husband, Dennis Fraschetti, who supported me in every out-of-town and out-of-country doctor appointment, and there were many! Thank you for encouraging my pilgrimages. I appreciate your patience and help during my first writing endeavour; I couldn't have accomplished my literary pursuit without you. I am grateful for you and all that you are. I love you forever and a day, yours truly.

To my wonderful daughter, Cynthia Fraschetti, who with candid assurance and simplicity, told me in her younger years, "Mom, you don't have to wait for a miracle to write a book. You can write one anyway!" Your belief and encouragement led me onto a new path. My journal evolved into a manuscript, in large part, due to your perspective. Whether I shared rough drafts of simple phrases, paragraphs, or chapters with you, your genuine interest was uplifting. Your empathy for my health struggles will always be treasured. Thank you for your sweetness. From the depths of my heart, I love you and your kind, savvy, and intuitive ways. I give you all my love, always and forever.

To my dear son, Bryan Fraschetti, who insightfully and foreknowingly, advised me on my medical dilemma: "Mom, you should stop searching on the internet for an answer. The computer doesn't know. Only God knows." At six years of age, you were right. From the depths of my soul, I love you, your wisdom, goodness, and compassion. Your loving, sensitive, and forgiving heart has captured mine. Thank you for your encouragement when I need it most. I will remain forever grateful for your instrumental role in helping me with my book and that you *saved the day* many times when I encountered numerous technical issues. With all my love, always and forever.

To my mother, Severina Pilon, and deceased father, Louis Pilon—whom I miss very much—thank you for your love and endless support that you've provided throughout my life. There aren't enough words to express my appreciation for all you have done for me and continue to do for my family. We are fortunate to have you in our lives. With much love.

To my sister and best friend, Michelle Doucette, who has a very big heart and always brings laughter and light to a situation. I'm forever blessed to have you by my side. Words would only prove inadequate to express my gratitude for you and your willingness to always be there for me, whether you're near or far away. Know that you hold a special place in my heart.

To my brother-in-law, Joe Doucette, and my nieces, Kelsey and Alyssa Doucette, I appreciate all of you. Thank you for your kindness, authentic affection, prayers, and concern for me. I return to you an overflowing cup of love.

To my extended family and valued friends who have shown an abundance of care. Thank you for your prayers, thoughtfulness, rays of sunshine, and companionship. I hope I reciprocate the same.

To Nina Williams, for introducing me to Saint Thérèse that fateful day! To her husband, Bob Williams, for suggesting I seek spiritual counsel with Father Beaune. Thank you both for your prayers, understanding, and all your expressions of faith and friendship. With affection.

To Father Beaune, my past spiritual adviser who resides with the Lord. Thank you for being an inspiration to me and countless others, and for effortlessly sharing your love and knowledge of God, the saints, and scripture. I will always remain appreciative for the time we shared.

To Maureen O'Riordan, curator of the invaluable website Saint Therese of Lisieux: A Gateway at http://www.thereseoflisieux. org/. Your devotion to Saint Thérèse, everything you have written and compiled about her, and your relentless professional work in making her known is exemplary. You have helped thousands of people along their spiritual journey. Thank you for your dedication and kindness.

To Sister Briege McKenna, thank you for taking the time during your very busy schedule to read excerpts from my book. I cherish your kind-hearted response to my request and appreciate you granting me permission to write about you and our encounter at your retreat.

To Monique Pilú and her husband Roger Pilú, thank you for hand delivering my letter to the French monsignor and for your effort to remain in touch over the years. Meeting you was no coincidence. I trust we shall see each other again. To Eric Pilú, thank you for kindly relaying my email messages to your parents, thus, facilitating our correspondence.

I am grateful to the many wonderful people who responded to my queries: librarians; bloggers; customer service representatives in the publishing industry; executive copyright holders; permissions managers; archivists; executive assistants to authors, doctors, and theologians; and priests and authors, themselves. Thank you for sharing your knowledge and generously giving of your time.

To Leanne Janzen and Oluwanifemi Okeowo, my publishing specialists at FriesenPress, thank you for your expert and patient guidance throughout the publishing process. I feel fortunate that you oversaw my project and will remain grateful for your exceptional support and enthusiastic encouragement regarding my book. Thank you to my entire team for helping me make my dream a reality.

To Matthew Fukushima, first and foremost, thank you for your gift of friendship—it's a treasure I hold dear to my heart. Thank you for giving freely of your time whenever it was needed. Your academic knowledge and assistance with my book were valued and appreciated.

To my warrior friend, whom I shall call Quinn, who valiantly went to her eternal home. You were a courageous soul whom I knew too briefly. Your pure excitement about my writing and the events in my life with the saints was unsurpassed. Your respect and sensitivity toward me, and others, will always be remembered.

ACKNOWLEDGEMENTS

A heartfelt thank you to Della Witt. Upon realizing that my efforts to assist you with your medical dilemmas by providing resources and therapeutic suggestions weren't enough, I intuitively offered glimpses of my experiences with Saint Thérèse of Lisieux. Your awe and sincere interest in my story, along with your curiosity in learning about Saint Thérèse, revived my dormant desire to pursue publishing my spiritual memoir. For this, I remain forever grateful.

Last, but not least, to Dana Kathryn—Della's sister—thank you for your outpouring of love and prayers. I will never forget your palpable enthusiasm about my angel story and manuscript. Just when I needed encouragement, you unknowingly sent me beautifully recorded messages that made me smile, lifted my spirits, and warmed my heart from afar. I look forward to meeting you both in person one day.

Preface

When does faith arise? Does it come from a yearning that emerges from trials and despair? Does it manifest from an innate void when one realizes that this emptiness cannot be filled but through God? Or does it simply exist for some fortunate souls at an early age? Its origins aren't paramount because, in the end, everyone has their own celebrated story.

Born Roman Catholic, I attended mass, made the sacraments, was familiar with a few biblical stories, and in my pre-teens questioned why I couldn't just pray at home instead of at church. I believed in God, felt that the beauty in the world came from Him, and prayed nightly. I enjoyed listening to my mother's story of how she beseeched Saint Bernadette of Lourdes to intercede on my behalf so that I may survive my birth.

At a very young age, I had a spectacular dream: for a brief and glorious moment, I was in the presence of God and three angels. I was immersed in the purest white light, embraced by celestial music, and inundated with limitless, sublime peace that permeated my surroundings as the Lord spoke to me. No matter how hard I tried, I couldn't perceive His faint words. For a long time afterwards, I went to sleep begging that He grant me this exact dream again. I arduously wanted to be able to decipher His message while feeling, once more, that infinite flood of serenity.

My faith was always honest and simple, and at times, remote and inconsiderable when, for days and years, I became disconnected from God. Reflecting on my life, I realized that I didn't always comprehend the small and large miracles showered upon me—not even those of grandeur, like the time when an angel descended before me in human form as an aged, curved beggar. Cloaked in tattered, grey, wool clothing with a matching frayed knitted tuque nestled just above her squinted blue eyes, she looked at me pleadingly. Her empty, humble hands were wrapped in shredded knit hobo gloves. I wish I had understood at the time who she was and held her hands in mine with warm recognition. On a desolate pathway, she mysteriously appeared out of nowhere, then disappeared, after saving me from a menacing Frenchman! The pale, grey moon even seemed to hide behind sparse clouds that late shivery December night. The brief and extraordinary encounter left me baffled. It wasn't until twenty-three years later that I realized she was a disguised angel from Heaven. Surely there are other moments of grace that I have yet, if ever, to discern.

Holding a thin stack of plain paper, with the sleeves of my sweater pulled down almost to my knuckles, pen in hand, I sat under the golden autumn sun and began to write about a miraculous occurrence that transpired at the Grotto Massabielle. I needed to express in words the indelible memory etched on my mind. Through squiggled passages, I recounted this exceptional life-changing event. Filtering through my trials, thoughts, and emotions, I unexpectedly continued to write and write. As the years passed, my journal gradually evolved into a manuscript.

My quest to find a resolution for my physical illnesses led me on a sacred journey where I not only searched for healing of mind, body, and soul, but unforeseeably sought salvation. Through contemplating both the wisdom imparted by Saint Thérèse of Lisieux and the power and truth that emerge from devout, earnest, and attentive prayer, I learned not only to have gratitude for what is seen and unseen but came to understand that *there is grace in all circumstances.*

As you flip through the pages and travel alongside me, may you grow in love, knowledge, and admiration for Saint Thérèse of Lisieux. Whether you already know her as a heavenly friend or have never heard of her before, I hope you will be amazed and feel inspired by the events in my life when her love and powerful intercession helped guide me. She is unfailing like the God she dearly loves. By telling my story, I aspire to provide hope for the weary and disheartened, bring eagerness to those on the verge of discovering their faith, and enkindle a desire in the pilgrim reader to turn to the angels and saints, who willingly assist us in our earthly and spiritual needs.

I assure you that once you turn wholeheartedly to God, it won't be long before you start experiencing the miraculous, for you are and will forever be under His divine gaze.

Call upon me in the day of trouble;
I will deliver you, and you will honor me.

Psalm 50:15

Lourdes, September 2006

My spiritual journey began long ago, before I had any remote awareness of how powerful it would inevitably become.

A search for a medical solution to a problem I had initially self-diagnosed became a daunting quest—one that I would not abandon until I was convinced it was attained. Years—eight to be exact—of looking for the right doctor, the right test, the right diagnosis, consumed me and led me to roads of confusion, frustration, anger, and temporary resignation. But they also filled me with patience, perseverance, determination, and a new-found assertiveness. Hope sustained me. God's grace guided me along this roller-coaster ride of emotion and uncertainty. At one definitive point, I came to the realization that eventually God's plan would unravel and be made clear to me.

I had consulted with several specialists to discuss my progressive vascular disease, and not one presented me with a solution. They either had no opinion or warned me that I would die on the operating table. Eventually, I gave up on the medical field and turned to my faith in the Lord. Prayer began to deliver me in times of unrest and strengthen me in times of need. I knew wholeheartedly that the trials given to me had a purpose, and this seemed to ease my soul.

As I grew in my faith, so did my desire to go on a pilgrimage to Lourdes, France. I longed to walk where Saint Bernadette Soubirous had once gathered wood by the stream, to pray near the spot where Mary had instructed her to kneel and eat grass—an act that dismayed the followers who had gathered around her—and to touch the stone wall of the Massabielle Grotto where she witnessed apparitions of the Immaculate Conception eighteen times. It became a necessity for me to personally experience this sacred place in the Pyrenean foothills.

My husband, Dennis, and I embarked on our first trip to France together. Upon arrival, I knew we were on holy ground. A sense of tranquility instantly washed over me. This feeling may have been due, in part, to unexpectedly seeing larger-than-life posters of Saint Bernadette decorating the airport terminal, which seemed to bless one's arrival. Looking out the ceiling-to-floor windows, I was captivated by an extraordinary view. The mauve and pink hues that sometimes accompany twilight reflected on the mountains. The colours looked embedded in the rock. The Pyrenees appeared stroked and graced by the hands of Monet, himself. The moment was enchanting and peaceful—a prophetic glimpse of the unimaginable life-changing experiences in store for me.

I recall looking through the glass walls that framed the room where our pilgrim group had gathered. The church bells tolled while I stared at the large, brilliant gilded cross and crown on top of the basilica. At this precise moment, our tour guide told us matter-of-factly, in a tone blended with spiritual depth, that "each one of us did not choose to come to Lourdes; we were called." My perception of why I was there began to change, and the first of many salty tears trickled down my face, warming my skin.

The following afternoon, we drank pure spring water from the mountain, which is accessible simply by turning on one of the many faucets stationed near the grotto. People were lined up in front of the row of spouts. While I celebrated the refreshing ice-cold water splashing onto my hands, I heard an announcement over the PA system that 10,000 people were en route from across Europe and would be arriving by train that day. I imagined an aerial view of these trains filled with passengers converging on the town. Upon witnessing thousands of visitors walking about, I began to wonder about many of them. *Had they arrived in hope of experiencing some personal transformation or were they accompanying a loved one in need?* Almost immediately, I found myself praying for these strangers instead of for myself. Since I had gone in desperate need of searching for answers to my own problems, I had not anticipated that I would have reacted the way that I did. My pleas, however, were a natural response to the overwhelming circumstance in which I found myself. For three days, I prayed for the pilgrims I saw, abandoning my own desires and needs because, at that point, I had completely lost the ability to ask for anything for myself.

The most unforgettable moment occurred around 2:00 a.m. on the morning of our departure. Hundreds of stars sparkled and the moon gleamed against a velvet sky. The view was dazzling. The sound of faint footsteps and soft voices accompanied the few lingering and praying pilgrims. I walked alongside the grotto, touching the rock, which seemed ageless and strong. Perhaps I did this to feel a connection with its strength, and to its past. Whenever in Europe, I am drawn to press my hands against a medieval door or a Roman pillar, to sense its antiquity. Earnestly, I studied the mountain rock and its formation under the night sky. A power drew me to stop and pray at a particular spot; it was there where I began the most intense moments of prayer I had ever known.

I leaned completely onto the rock, arms bent and extended over my head. Praying with my whole heart, I called out to the Lord for those at war, for family, and friends. I was not crying; I was weeping in prayer. Never before had I experienced this dimension of humility, submission, or invocation. I didn't know how to begin to pray for my own intentions because my journey as a pilgrim naturally made me forget myself. I was about to present my personal request to Mary when, just before doing so, I received a beautiful and undeniable sign.

The palms of my hands started to feel damp, as did my arms. Then, they began to feel increasingly wet. Confused, I looked downwards and noticed my clothes were strangely becoming streaked with water. I couldn't reason clearly. I looked again at where my hands were placed and saw water flowing slowly but steadily out of the rock. In an attempt to comprehend what was happening, my eyes quickly darted around the grotto: most areas of the rock in my vicinity were glistening with moisture. Nowhere else, other than where my hands were placed, was water coming out of the rock. When I began to realize the magnitude of what was happening, the water gurgled faster and faster out of the rock onto me, symbolic of my gushing tears. My pants became saturated in sacred water. I stepped backwards to look up to the heavens to thank and praise the Lord for this indisputable sign. I realized, then, that the entire time I had been praying I was unknowingly standing directly beneath the illuminated statue of the Madonna. This niche, where the apparitions had appeared to Saint Bernadette 148 years before, instantly took on a unique personal significance.

I looked upwards into the eyes of the statue. Mary, the mother of God, then spoke to me. With compassion, she revealed to my heart: *I understand.* My heart was full and at rest. I was blessed with a profound awareness and sweet consolation: she knew my most intimate thoughts and needs. Nothing else mattered.

*Be Still before the Lord
and wait patiently for him.*[1]

Psalm 37:7a

Rome, September 2006

Our return flight from Lourdes to Rome was shared with fellow pilgrims who came from across Italy; it was a harmonious experience both in camaraderie and in sound. Quietly and amicably, the passengers spoke to one another as they settled into their seats and awaited takeoff. The cadence of their voices was melodic and sounded like a beautiful Italian song. The murmuring was serene and soothing like that of a babbling brook in the

---

[1] The Bible verses in the chapter epigraphs reference God as "him," or "he." Pronouns are not capitalized because translators for NIV, "decided that fidelity to the original was their highest criterion." "The Greek does not use upper case in employing these pronouns, and Hebrew uses only capital letters and has no lowercase letters." – Biblica, Publisher of the NIV

distance. I kept to myself and thought about the many special blessings received during our four-day stay in Lourdes.

I looked through the small, slightly scratched, oval window with its spotted residue of raindrops. While glancing at the majestic mountains one last time, I whispered a sentimental farewell to a town where I felt ineffable peace. Whenever I travel, I look forward to the adventures that await me. When I leave, the discoveries and memories made settle inside me and are preserved for further reflection, inspiration, and gratitude.

The physical cure I had originally hoped for was not provided. It took time for me to realize the depth of the gifts I had received in its place: the sanctified pilgrimage, the supernatural sign, and the celestial message given to me by Mary at the grotto. This was the beginning of a spiritual journey that would take hold of my life in unparalleled ways.

Mother Mary and Saint Bernadette collaborated quickly on my behalf! On our flight to Rome, I had an invaluable encounter. I met a woman who provided me with the name of the Chief of Vascular Surgery at a well-recognized institution in Rome—the Policlinico Umberto I. Though knowledge of this specialist came towards the end of my sojourn in Italy, I managed to visit briefly with him the day before our departure home to Canada. After further correspondence, I returned to the Eternal City a year later to discuss his proposed means of intervention. The several required surgeries were a radical approach that caused me to feel unsure. It is said that all roads lead to Rome; well, I had arrived but was no longer convinced I was on the right path. I wondered, though, *how couldn't I be?*

The only doctor who had ever offered me a solution was the one I had met through a connection from Lourdes. Did I need to veer off the Appian Way? I desperately wanted healing, yet I felt like my search was approaching a dead end—a destination I certainly wasn't ready to accept. My heart recited words of not giving up. I realized Saint Bernadette, whom my mother had called upon when I almost died at birth, had been with me for a long time. It was as though she knew I would answer her call some forty years later.

I needed direction but never fathomed how much, nor that another saint would soon enter my life. Oh, what rich blessings were to come my way! Through my trials, His plans began to slowly unveil before my soul.

Lord, help me!

Matthew 15:25b

Back to Him

During the process of searching for help, I suffered interiorly on different levels. My heart ached unceasingly. Over time, I learned this truth: "How else but through a broken heart may the Lord Christ enter in?" (Oscar Wilde)[2]

At times, I felt lost and grew weary of hoping and waiting. The delay in receiving answers about my disease was an obvious test. How much did I really trust in the Lord? Longing for a divine sustaining force, I prayed more intently, which drew me closer to God. During this time, I was acutely aware that He was calling me back to Him.

---

[2]   Wilde, Oscar. "The Ballad of Reading Gaol" Accessed May 16, 2022. https://poets.org/poem/ballad-reading-goal.

One morning, something unsuspected happened that changed my life forever. I explained to a colleague and friend that it was completely impossible for me to decide whether or not I should have surgery in Rome. Clearly, I greatly desired a solution and going to Italy for treatment was, without a doubt, alluring in more ways than one. At a standstill, I wanted God to come down from Heaven and just tell me what to do. Perhaps my confidant read my mind. She looked over at me, reached for my hand, and directed me towards a small photo on her office wall. With assurance and a twinkle in her eye, she responded most confidently: "Ask Saint Thérèse. She'll tell you what you should do!"

Astonished at such a claim, I replied: "Who? Nina, what are you talking about?"

From that moment, my intrigue about this beloved saint began.

If God answers my requests,
my heaven will be spent on earth
up until the end of the world.

Saint Thérèse

Florida, March 2008

Saint Thérèse of Lisieux is known the world over for her spirituality, answering prayer requests, and helping souls obtain miracles—and yet I had never heard of her. The stories my friend shared about Saint Thérèse's intercession were simply fascinating. Not for an instant did I doubt the possibility that she would give a physical sign to those who prayed to her in need. I went home to contemplate if I was ready to pray a powerful novena, a nine-day prayer of invocation that millions of people claim she answers. *Was I prepared for her to intercede on my behalf? Would I be willing to accept the answer that she would provide?*

For days, I continuously thought and wondered about Thérèse Martin, the young woman from a small village in France. Late one afternoon, while walking down the video aisle at Walmart, I glanced at the DVDs and, to my surprise, the entire section was a blur. Only one stood out vividly and distinctly. The cover had an image of fluttering crimson rose petals on a white background and was entitled *Thérèse*! It was no coincidence that it captured my attention in such a dramatic fashion. Naturally, I bought the movie. With excitement, I immediately went home to watch it and become more familiar with her life story. That night, I decided that I was ready to begin my first novena.

My relationship with this phenomenal saint, who lived an ordinary life, would soon blossom and flourish. One of her missions is to bring people closer to God. When invoked, Saint Thérèse, the "Little Flower of Jesus," answers prayers by sending her signature sign—a rose—or other flowers and manifestations. Whenever I'd call upon her for guidance, I'd receive a bouquet. My prayer requests were exacting. I wanted her signs to be crystalline, leaving no doubt in my mind as to the answers given. I beseeched her to obtain for me from God the favour of receiving "fresh-cut pink tulips in a vase, not a pot, if I should have the surgeries." I envisioned the exact colour and asked that they be delivered directly into my hands. No one knew of my prayer request. I felt confident that she could meet my expectations. All that was required from me was faith, trust, patience, and the will of God.

One evening while vacationing in Florida, my parents, my children, Cynthia and Bryan, and I met at a friend's house for dinner. I waited on the driveway for my parents to arrive. I was shocked and amazed to see my mother get out of the car embracing a large pot of pink tulips. It was the ninth and last day of my novena. Perplexed, I remained frozen in disbelief. Silently, I started to chat with my Little Flower and explained quite frankly,

Saint Thérèse, I asked that I'd receive them in a vase. These are in a pot; they aren't in a vase, and I am sorry, it just won't do.

My mother then held them right in front of me, at the level of my chin. I could faintly smell the soil. She looked me in the eyes, walked right by me, and said in a tone that seemed abrupt at the time, "These aren't for you—they're for the hostess!" Pot in hand, she hustled away.

I stood there alone under the warmth of the sun's rays. The palm leaves swayed, gently rustling in the breeze. Entranced, I tried to figure out what had just transpired. The tulips were the precise shade of pink I desired. They were even partially closed, just as I prefer them, despite that I had never openly expressed this to my Little Flower. But they were in a pot, and I didn't receive them. Reflecting, I went to her in prayer. This cryptic message then became clear: Saint Thérèse did hear me! The tulips were shown to me, but I didn't receive them because she wasn't ready to provide the answer. I understood that I was meant to keep on praying and be assured that she was there, listening! This moment of sensing her presence in my life felt enormous and seized my heart.

Since it wasn't the right time for me to receive the answer, I decided to engage in twenty-four-days of supplication to honour the number of years she had lived. During this time, as my circumstances changed, so did my need for direction.

Prior to learning about Saint Thérèse, I had contacted a distinguished vascular surgeon in Madrid. I shall refer to him as Dr. Romero. His name would often appear attached to the studies and journals I had extensively read regarding my health problems. Before starting my first novena, I had written him an email with the hope that he would respond and shed further light on my situation, thus assisting me with my decision about the

Italian surgeon's approach. Whenever I messaged him, he replied the same day. With his approval, I sent him a hard copy of my diagnostic images by post, which he reviewed with his associates. He contacted me while I was still on holiday in Florida, shortly after I had finished my nine-day novena. He spoke of likely being able to help me, but via a different means than that proposed by the Italian doctor. With this turn of events, I realized that had I received the tulips, I would have remained confused as to which path to pursue, since I now had two surgeons claiming that they could help me.

It was time to call upon Saint Thérèse in fervent prayer.

She surely listened to my pleas and "let fall a shower of roses,"[3] fulfilling her mission in remarkable and undeniable ways. Through her, I learned that peace can be found when I surrender my trials and myself in complete abandonment to the Lord, especially when the answers I receive are not in accordance with my heart's desire.

---

[3]   Thérèse of Lisieux (Saint), *Story of a Soul: The Autobiography of St. Thérèse of Lisieux*, ed. Mother Agnes of Jesus, trans. Michael Day, (Rockford, IL: TAN Books and Publishers, 1997), 213.

Your prayer has been heard.

Luke 1:13a

Home

I needed and sought divine intercession. Being a mother and having two young children made it completely impossible for me to make such an important health decision on my own. Guidance and a message from Heaven were in order. Saint Thérèse would act as my mediator and, with my tremendous trust and belief in her, our journey together would begin. With delight and laughter, I began to receive more flowers in response to my novenas. On such occasions, I'd sometimes laugh until I cried. I was overtaken by her presence, her love that surrounded me, and the fulfillment of her promise. She was there with me, real and alive. I did wonder *how anyone could not believe in these occurrences.*

I invoked Saint Thérèse requesting gerbera daisies if I should pursue a trip to Spain. I envisioned a variety of colours and the type of bouquet itself. Never did I question her ability to provide a specific flower with precision—if it was meant to be granted, it would be. I only petitioned my Little Flower when I felt I would be emotionally prepared to receive an answer I truthfully did not want.

The first evening after having started this novena, I heard a measured, pleasing tap at our front door. Unsure who it could be at that hour, I peered through our small, bevelled glass door window. The silvery moonlight beamed behind my friend who nonchalantly stood at the doorstep. The porch light cast an amber hue upon her. She held a wrapped gift and explained that she had been at the store and thought of me. Cautiously, I loosened the crinkled metallic, fuchsia-coloured paper while listening intently to its crisp, crackling sound. Large gerbera daisies! They were exactly all the colours I had requested. The message was clear: I was heard and being guided from above! Overjoyed, I shared the news with my family. My children were in awe, their eyes bright with wonder. The stars sparkled brightly upon us that evening.

Hopeful and encouraged, I made all the necessary arrangements for my mother and I to fly to Madrid to meet world-renowned specialist, Dr. Romero. Oddly enough, I still desired to receive one more affirmation that I had made the right decision. This time, I spoke with urgency: "Okay, Saint Thérèse, I need some flowers, and I need them fast! This time, I don't care what kind, what colour, just make it fast—real fast!" Within half an hour, my adorable daughter went to the backyard and gathered a lovely, small handful of wild violets and handed them to me. She reminded me of how Saint Thérèse loved nature and had collected flowers as a little girl.

Shortly thereafter, I dropped my daughter off at school. I continued on to do some errands when, while driving, I realized I had forgotten my wallet. I returned home and saw a delivery van parked on the opposite side of the street, across from my house. The words FLOWER DELIVERY were painted in unusually large, bold, white letters across the entire side of the forest green van. My heart pounded with anticipation. My mind raced with curiosity. I tried to bury the fact that I wasn't completely convinced with the hand-picked spring blooms I had received earlier, meaningful as they were. My dear Saint Thérèse was aware of my inner thoughts that I needed a more telling floral arrangement.

As I got out of my car, the man got out of his van. I moved with trepidation. He, instead, walked with a hastened pace towards me. With energy and assurance, he quickly placed an enormous vase into my hands; only then did he ask if I wouldn't mind giving it to my neighbours. The interesting fact is that I had just passed them on the road before I had entered my driveway. The delivery man and my neighbours had just missed each other, and I wasn't even supposed to be home. It felt like a twist of fate, each event being manoeuvred from above. Since my neighbours had gone out of town for a few days, this spectacular arrangement remained in my home. The way in which I received this sign was a striking reminder of God's love and power, from which all things come. Again, I was enchanted by Saint Thérèse's unique way of answering my requests. I also noticed her sense of humour in that not only was the mix of flowers of various shades brought to me with such speed, but they were delivered in such an animated way!

I once read that flowers received through Saint Thérèse's intercession had to be blessed first by the Lord. I couldn't be more certain I was on the right path. Most importantly, I felt I would somehow be prepared to accept the outcome, whatever it might be. I was thrilled and comforted to have her by my side.

It is a mistake to look too far ahead.
The chain of destiny can only be grasped
one link at a time.

Winston Churchill

Bound for Madrid, June 2008

I left for Madrid knowing that I was fulfilling my destiny, which made the voyage seem surreal. Years earlier, when I intensively researched my health problems, I was repeatedly drawn to Dr. Romero's work. I never would have imagined randomly telling my family then that *I wanted to go to Spain to see a specialist I read about,* even though I had thought about it. God's plan became clearer: Lourdes led me to Rome—not only to lead me to Madrid but also so that Saint Thérèse would accompany me on my journey. This was a rich blessing!

On the plane ride, much to my bewilderment, the start of many signs connecting me to Saint Thérèse began. What were the chances that while flying overseas, I would watch a movie depicting the re-enactment of a few miracles through our Little Flower's intercession? The film *La Vie en Rose* was projected from the large centre screen. I didn't expect to watch a foreign film about Edith Piaf—a French singer who prayed wholeheartedly to Saint Thérèse. I was familiar with a few of her famous songs but not her tragic, compelling life story.

Born in a poor district of Paris, Edith is abandoned at a young age. Her mother, a destitute street performer, informs her husband, a circus acrobat, that she is leaving their daughter with her mother so that she can pursue her singing career. He receives news of her decision via a letter while he is fighting in World War I. He returns to find Edith neglected and immediately removes her from her grandmother's wretched care—only to leave her with his own mother who runs a brothel in Normandy—and then returns to fight in the war.

Little Edith is loved by the prostitutes who raise her. Her vision begins to decline at around three years of age. One evening, she tells them that she can't see. The following day, a doctor diagnoses her with keratitis—an inflammation of the cornea. Heartbroken and hoping for a miracle, the prostitutes take her on a pilgrimage to Lisieux. While at the town cemetery, they plead to Saint Thérèse and "baby Jesus"[4] for her cure. Titine, who has spent the most time raising Edith, encourages her to speak to Saint Thérèse. Standing in front of Saint Thérèse's tomb with a cloth wrapped over her eyes, Edith tells her that she "doesn't want to be blind and wants to run and play like before."[4] A short time thereafter,

---

[4]   Olivier, Dahan, director. *La Vie en Rose*. Featuring Marion Cotillard. Légende Films, TF1 International, Canal+, TPS Star. 2007. 2 hr., 20 min.

her sight is restored. From that moment, she becomes devoted to Saint Thérèse for the rest of her life.

Deeply moved by the scene in which Edith was brought to the cemetery, a strong desire took hold of me! I began to dream of one day bowing down on my knees in prayer at the cemetery of Lisieux. I envisioned myself there, on hallowed ground. With a sense of marvel, I lifted my prayer to Heaven, hopeful that one day such good fortune would come my way.

As we disembarked, the steward expressively handed my mother and me each a rose—Saint Thérèse's symbol! I had previously flown on fifty-two flights and never received a flower while on board a plane. Without a doubt, something mysterious was in the air. Signs were appearing without my request, and this filled me with great wonder.

Be joyful in hope,
patient in affliction,
faithful in prayer.

Romans 12:12

Madrid, June 2008

Dr. Romero worked in a private clinic on the outskirts of Madrid. The cafeteria staff served frothy lattes and freshly squeezed orange juice. They also used fragrant olive oil in their nutritious meal preparations. I thought of how pleasant it would be to recover in a hospital where wholesome food is provided. Given my first impressions and the quality of the overall service I received, it was not surprising that the then Prince and Princess of Asturias, now King Felipe VI and Queen Letizia of Spain, chose to have their daughters delivered at this remarkable clinic.

When I met Dr. Romero, I learned that he had discussed my case with his team of fifteen doctors prior to my arrival. I was their first Canadian patient. They treated me with keen interest, kindness, and compassion. I immediately felt at ease with this highly skilled, extremely intelligent, yet down-to-earth doctor. After performing a thorough clinical examination, he ordered a diagnostic test that I had never had before. I had read that Pelvic Venous Congestion Syndrome (PVCS) could be secondary to more serious underlying pathologies—May-Thurner Syndrome (MTS), Nutcracker Syndrome (NCS), or both. These rare conditions were finally acknowledged and would be investigated for the first time.

Many large posters and charts depicting elaborate studies covered the walls of the waiting room. I tried to interpret a few of them by looking at the images, arrows, and reading the Spanish words that resembled either the Italian or French language. As I waited to speak with the receptionist, the cliché, *you're exactly where you're meant to be*, took on real significance. For the first time in my life, I experienced the depth of this saying in a profound way. I had an astonishing sense that I was precisely where God wanted me to be. An extraordinary awareness descended upon me, and an inner calm pervaded in my soul. I knew that all the long years of searching had brought me here, exactly where I needed to be. I waited in silence and gratitude for my name to be called.

The test results indicated that I had MTS, which caused my PVCS and Chronic Venous Insufficiency (CVI). The doctor breathed a sigh of relief that NCS was ruled out. This new finding decidedly affected the method of treatment. The surgeon felt he could perform the necessary surgeries. Next, I needed to meet with a doctor from the Department of Anaesthesiology to confirm whether or not I was a candidate for the procedure since I was allergic to the required contrast dye. Dr. Romero's team of specialists would confer with one another to further discuss my case.

Before leaving for Spain, I had often invoked Saint Thérèse to send me a single yellow rose if, while in Madrid, I should risk being administered contrast dye in the event that it would be deemed necessary. I didn't receive the flower; however, it was clear to me that it wasn't yet the right time for the answer to be revealed. I petitioned my dear saint, requesting once more that I receive a single yellow rose. Throughout the entire day, I called upon her for guidance and spoke to her right up until I walked through the anaesthesiologist's office door. The moment had arrived for me to receive their opinion. Since I was considered a high-risk patient due to my complicated medical history and several life-threatening drug allergies, the doctors' plans included additional precautionary steps—ones that no other facility ever proposed. The operating room would be shut down for two full days and large signs, the size of the windows, would be posted on all of them: No Latex. These measures would ensure sterilization and elimination of latex particles that could still be floating in the air forty-eight hours after having been used in the room. Their approach made me feel like royalty. But were these safety measures enough? All my concerns were discussed comprehensively. The developments did not seem promising. Feelings of disappointment fluttered through me. It was our third day in Europe, and the thought of my quest being over without a resolution seemed probable. The assistant doctor would now need to confer with the Chief of Anaesthesiology, and I was to meet Dr. Romero the next day.

While standing in the office waiting room, ready to schedule my follow-up appointment, I was taken by great surprise: a single yellow rose lay on the secretary's desk! It wasn't there when I had passed through the room prior to entering the doctor's office. I knew Saint Thérèse couldn't provide a sign until I had spoken with all the specialists. A premature answer from her would have been pointless; first, I needed to hear their professional opinion. I stared at the rose in true bewilderment, wondering if for some strange and beautiful reason someone would present it to me. I deliberately peered at the delicate petals, then glanced at my surroundings and the few people seated in the room. Everyone around me appeared to be moving in slow motion. Sounds became muffled and almost inaudible. It felt like I'd entered a time warp. Suddenly, everything quickly zapped back to normal.

I waited, staring at the lonely rose that remained on the countertop. Full of want, I paused a moment longer. With empty hands and hope grown forlorn, I shuffled my purse over my shoulder, gathered my medical file, and prepared myself to leave.

I left the room slightly dazed.

My mother and I then proceeded to Dr. Romero's office so that I could offer him a present in appreciation for his efforts in helping me. He was not there. Instead, we saw the Department Head of Anaesthesiology and the second doctor in command. They were speaking with his secretary. This unexpected encounter surprised us all. They, too, were looking for him to discuss my case. Our paths had crossed perfectly for this *chance meeting*. Energy filled the room as we all looked at each other, happy to have an impromptu consultation. Much time and commitment were given to discussing my medical dilemma. I could not have asked for greater expertise, dedication, or timing of events.

They concluded, to everyone's displeasure, that I was considered "too high-risk" and not a candidate for any type of procedure. With a slightly faint heart and in a dreamlike state, I left Hospital Ruber Internacional very, very quietly.

To limit your desires and your hopes
is to misunderstand God's infinite goodness.

Saint Thérèse

Hospital Ruber Internacional

The next day, we went to bid farewell to Dr. Romero and his colleagues. He referred to me as being someone of "great importance." Made to feel like a queen again, I smiled at him most graciously.

With kind regard, he told me that no matter where I searched— Brazil, Japan, anywhere—I would be told the same thing. He advised me most tenderly that I must now stop searching. He knew I had searched relentlessly for help in Canada, Italy, and the United States. My determined nature did not allow me to give up. From behind his desk, he slowly leaned forward and divulged in a soft whispery tone, "You see *la vie en rose.*" He spoke these words with a forced, reluctant smile as he sympathetically shook his head from side to side. He clearly conveyed his regretful underlying

29

message that life just isn't always that way—rosy, perfect and the way I wish it would be. He wanted me to be realistic and, yet, also remember the infinite possibilities that are born out of one's faith. Never had I met a physician who referenced the benefits of spiritual beliefs. I was fortunate to have met this grand and gentle soul.

My mother and I decided to go to the cafeteria for one last creamy coffee—a *café con leche*. Dr. Romero's youngest assistant, who had also sometimes acted as our translator, happened to be there. Silently, he stood next to me in line. He looked at me with deep regret and honest sorrow. His expressive, brown eyes conveyed that he truly wished that their medical team could have helped me. I left feeling his compassion in my heart, and this eased my departure.

It is the way of the spiritual childhood,
the way of truſt and absolute surrender.

Saint Thérèse

Calle Santa Teresa

Being in Madrid felt more surreal than ever as we wandered the streets looking for a tapas bar. For the first time during our excursions downtown, my mother directed our way. She wanted to go here, then there, then there and here, and although I was interiorly annoyed with her unmethodical route, I patiently agreed. Not to my surprise, she managed to navigate us outside the city centre.

We roamed down a boulevard with high, arched trees. She hesitantly whispered an uncharacteristic sentiment: "Monique, I feel like Saint Thérèse is with us now." She then looked upwards where the trees' canopy dispersed. Speechless, she stopped. I looked at her fixed expression then followed the direction of her sparkling eyes. The street sign read: *Calle Santa Teresa*. Instantly, our hands locked, and we gingerly turned the street corner. Laughing, we looked at one other and said in unison, "Forget the tapas!" Our pace quickened with excitement.

As we walked down the narrow cobblestone street, with reservation and curiosity, my mother said sotto voce, "I wonder if we'll get another sign?" Immediately after she spoke these words, we found ourselves standing in front of *Ristorante Nuovo Santa Teresa*! With over four thousand bars, cafes, and restaurants in Madrid, it was no coincidence that we happened upon it. A heavenly force had guided us there. No other explanation was plausible. Even with a map, we would have had a difficult time finding this nestled little place.

Slowly, we entered the restaurant, which was family operated and clearly frequented by the locals. A young girl was quietly tending to her homework in front of the wood-burning pizza oven with its coals glowing orange. Enticing aromas filtered out from the kitchen. The lighting was dim. The atmosphere was cozy, modest, and inviting. The mood was intimate and unpretentious. Maybe eight tables furnished the room. A middle-aged gentleman, who was reading the newspaper through retro spectacles, occupied one of them. He looked like a regular. Everything was authentic about this setting. Even the fresh olives were home-grown in their small courtyard and, notably, the best I had ever tasted. Everything was magical; it felt like we had entered the scene of an old, foreign film.

With reverence, we marvelled at the picture of *Santa Teresa* on the wall, a physical reminder of her presence; metaphorically, she was watching over us. I was deeply moved by her love for me. The peace I felt that evening cannot be described.

The evening of the 9th of June, after brilliant doctors told me they couldn't help me, I did not crumble. I was not sad. Under ordinary circumstances, this would be unthinkable. The only tears I shed were of joy and of self-abandonment to the Lord. It was providential: Santa Teresa was with me, along with a loving, merciful God who sent her to me and from whom I could draw strength. The unfolding events of the day were pivotal. After all the years of searching for answers, I was finally ready for complete surrender. I knew with absolute conviction that my long road of searching had come to its end. I had no control over my situation. Although the outcome was not that for which I had longed, a mysterious calm took hold of me—entirely. A serene melody sang in my heart. Yet, for an unfamiliar reason, I felt that my story was still not over.

In the preceding years, during which I had felt weary, doubtful, and uncertain, I turned to God. Out of tremendous need, I sought Him tenaciously and pleaded for His saving grace. I learned that true persistence in prayer and trust in the Lord must not be forsaken. His power and that of His favoured saints were revealed to me.

The 9th of June was the dawn of a new era in my spiritual journey. That celebrated evening, I received a purity of knowledge of His sustaining presence—an awareness that I wished could remain with me constantly and forever. I was awakened to a luminous path, one on which I began to search for God in everything.

Everything is a grace!

Saint Thérèse

Reflections of the Heart

Over the next year, I grasped both the depth of Saint Thérèse's words, "Everything is a grace!"[5] and the following reflection based upon that belief: "Everything is the direct effect of our Father's love—difficulties, contradictions, humiliations, all the soul's miseries, her burdens, her needs—everything, because through them, she learns humility, realizes her weakness. Everything is a grace because everything is God's gift. Whatever be the character

  [5]   Thérèse of Lisieux (Saint), *Story of a Soul: The Autobiography of St. Thérèse of Lisieux*, trans. John Clarke, third edition (Washington, DC: ICS Publications, 1996), 266.

of life or its unexpected events, to the heart that loves, all is well."[6,7]
I attribute much of my intense spiritual growth to Saint
Thérèse. When I first learned of her, I felt an immediate affinity.
I became increasingly united with her and spoke to her in
confidence numerous times throughout the day. Sometimes, I
prayed her novena incessantly. I read many books related to her
and was inspired by her message of love, hope, and charity. My
faith grew in innumerable ways as a result of adopting her "way of
trust and absolute surrender."[8]

I drew upon her enlightenment. I became exceedingly grateful
that Saint Thérèse had entered my life. For the first time, I began
to thank the Lord for my illnesses because through them I was
brought to her. A simple thought of her would often bring me to
tears. I came to understand that my encounter with her was part
of God's plan all along. She was one of His hidden treasures that I
was meant to discover—an extravagant gift that my soul required!
When the extreme physical pain became difficult to endure, I was
able to accept my suffering because I had learned that there was
grace to be found in everything.

During the second winter after I met Saint Thérèse, I realized
how weak I was and how much I yearned for emotional salvation

---

[6]   Prayer card. The prayer card from which I originally read these words
seems to have been inspired by *The Spirituality of St. Thérèse: An Introduction* by
the esteemed theologian and historian, Abbé André Combes. While words in
his book are taken, rearranged, and somewhat changed, they keep with his
meaning and reflections. They were and remain an important contribution to
my spiritual awakening.

[7]   Abbé André Combes, *The Spirituality of St. Thérèse: An Introduction*
third printing edition New York, NY: P.J. Kennedy & Sons 1950), 149, 150.

[8]   Thérèse, *Story of a Soul*, third edition, xi.

in other areas of my life. Winter's cold, dreary days intensified my feelings of hopelessness. One sombre and tearful afternoon, the snow fell heavily, and the bitter wind slashed against my window as I sat alone in undisclosed sadness, reflecting on my life.

I had become nothing.

I was nothing.

I took pleasure, however, in this realization and was content with my conclusion that I was weak and nothingness unto myself. My weakness did not frighten me; instead, I embraced it and welcomed it warmly. What a discovery: in my weakness I was strong, for my strength was finally found in Him.

Faith is being sure of what we hope for
And certain of what we do not see.

Hebrews 11:1

Hopes and Promises

Prayer nourished me, and I craved it daily. Continuous, unrelenting prayer became a part of my existence. I was in need of salvation, liberation, and purification. This thirst came from certain life challenges that seemed to mysteriously present themselves without forewarning. I was, thus, drawn more passionately to the Lord. My need for redemption cannot be described. I consoled my sometimes-shrunken soul with the assurance that one day He would answer my prayers. With unshaken faith, I insisted and pleaded that He hear my deepest needs and answer them. I kept Him accountable to His promises and assured Him that I would keep on waiting for Him.

As time passed, it became a necessity for me to walk in the footsteps of Saint Thérèse. I longed to see where she lived. I dreamt of breathing the seaside air of Normandy, jaunting over to Trouville for a day to see where she enjoyed spending her summers with her aunt, and visiting the beach that inspired Monet. I had an ardent desire to grab and firmly hold the soil from the cemetery, to smear it between my fingers. Ah, but my friend in Heaven, knowing of my secret suffering, must have looked down upon me with pity! She began to call me to her hometown in a more evident way, like Saint Bernadette had three years prior.

Soon I would embark on a personal pilgrimage. With heart-warming support, my husband, our children, and my parents encouraged me to pursue this trip. Each, in their own way, understood the importance of Saint Thérèse in my life and my need to travel to Lisieux.

Therefore I tell you,
whatever you ask for in prayer,
believe that you have received it,
and it will be yours.

Mark 11:24

9 June

Arrangements for my hotel, air transportation, and train ride from Paris to Lisieux were in order. I began to reminisce about my overseas flight to Spain. Never would I have imagined that a year later I would be going to France. Yes, God heard my incessant prayers, and through my trials, I did receive graces.

Rummaging through a folder of some stored items from my trip to Madrid, I came upon the bill from the memorable evening at Ristorante Nuevo Santa Teresa. I curiously unfolded the paper: *El 9 de junio 2008.* The 9th of June! I was mystified! Unbeknownst to me at the time of booking my trip to Lisieux, I had chosen the same date of departure as that of when we were divinely guided to the restaurant in Madrid. Yes, it was all meant to happen on this precise day. A year later, to the exact date of my self-abandonment to the Lord, I would leave for Normandy. I was beyond words.

I was awakened to the infinite possibilities that come from prayer. For eight long years, I had diligently searched for a doctor to help save me from a problem that had existed even longer. On the 9th of June, I knew my search was over. On that day, with Saint Thérèse by my side, I was finally able to completely surrender my quest and trials to the Lord. As I tightly held the preserved receipt, God's plan for me unravelled further—as three years before I believed it would someday.

Meanwhile, I continued to devour more books on Saint Thérèse. I was surprised to discover an entire chapter in the book, *With Empty Hands*, by Conrad de Meester, dedicated to the "solemn and privileged moment in her spiritual journey."[9] As Meester recounts, "[i]t was on 9 June 1895, to be exact—a bright, radiant spring morning and the feast of the Holy Trinity—that a marvellous meeting with the Lord took place in Thérèse's heart during the Eucharist. She suddenly received the grace to understand better than ever how much Jesus desires to be loved."[10]

In her autobiographical entry, on the 9th of June, Saint Thérèse offers herself to love, in her *Act of Oblation to Merciful*

---

[9]   Conrad De Meester, *With Empty Hands: The Message of St. Therese of Lisieux*, trans. Mary Seymour, (Washington, DC: ICS Publishing, 2002), 72.

[10]   Ibid., 71.

Love. On the same day that she claimed her "powerlessness"[11] I was able to surrender my trial to His will, thus, professing my powerlessness too. Since she considered the coinciding of dates to be of significance, the 9th of June felt even more meaningful.

Connecting to a divine and supreme power carries an incomparable awareness and happiness. A heavenly, magnificent force was at work in my life, and my eyes, heart, and soul were open to receive the Lord.

---

[11]   Lilles, A., & Burnes, D. October 1, 2018. *St. Thérèse's Act of Oblation to Merciful Love.* St. Paul Centre for Biblical Theology. Accessed May 31, 2022, https://stpaulcenter.com the-act-of-oblation-to-merciful-love/

The setting sun's last rays
were gilding the treetops
where birds were singing their evening prayer.

Saint Thérèse

Lisieux

I always adored exploring *la belle France* for its vast history, rich culture and tradition, quaint towns, splendid coastline, expansive countryside, magnificent châteaux, breathtaking beauty, exceptional wine, infamous baguettes, delectable pastries, irresistible chocolate, and abundant variety of cheeses. This time, however, my reason for travelling to France was born purely out of a longing to retrace Saint Thérèse's footsteps. I would still have to dine at least once at a fine French restaurant; it would be wrong to do otherwise. I would also have to walk down a charming old street somewhere, savouring a deliciously fresh baguette along the way, for this would make me feel very French. Apart from these two small indulgences, all I wished for was to experience: taking a tour of Saint Thérèse's second home as this would prove invaluable to my heart; visiting the Carmel where she spent the happiest years of her life; attending mass at both the Gothic cathedral where she worshipped and at the Roman-Byzantine basilica erected in her honour; and, of course, praying on my knees at the community cemetery where she was initially laid to rest.

The mere thought that one day I would wander through the streets of Lisieux filled me with optimism. I asked for a sign so that I would know if my desire was aligned with what God wanted. I had made an inquiry to the Sanctuaire de Lisieux regarding their guided tours and was then unexpectedly accepted to be a volunteer. My role would have been to welcome pilgrims, answer questions, and be a guide at the basilica and monastery for a few weeks. Due to the physical limitations associated with my health problems, I had to decline the offer but, through this sequence of events, I believed Saint Thérèse was calling me to visit her hometown. I was overjoyed that I'd be going to France and that she called me there.

From Paris's Charles de Gaulle airport I took a regional train—which connects the airport to the city centre—to the station Gare du Nord. I stepped outside to briefly appreciate its neoclassical façade with its twenty-three statues. I then took the underground passage to Gare Magenta and from there another commuter train to Gare Haussmann Saint-Lazare. Next, I again walked underground to Gare Paris-Saint-Lazare in the 8th *arrondissement*. While navigating my way, I was followed by two Frenchmen. A taxi ride would have been a much less complicated and more pleasing way to travel from the airport to the train station that serves northwestern France.

I wanted to take a moment to see the hustle and bustle of Parisienne life and the exterior architectural design of Gare-Saint-Lazare, the first train station built in Paris. A few impressionist artists—Manet, Caillebotte, and Monet—once lived near this historical building. Monet painted a dozen paintings of this station. When I returned inside, I intentionally stood on the passenger platform and looked up at the iron-glass rooftop. I was struck by its sheer size. I imagined the billowing blue smoke from the steam engines of days gone-by arriving from Normandy and Monet's depictions of this popular motif shared by many Impressionists.

I have always enjoyed the poetic atmosphere and ambient sounds at a European railway station. The trains in France were sleek and modern, unlike the ones I had taken back home. After a long voyage from Canada and having to evade the troublesome men who were following me, I welcomed having a seat in first class. I was now safe in a quiet compartment, travelling comfortably through the picturesque countryside.

A self-assured older businessman sat across from me. A table lamp emitting a warm glow, his grey laptop, ebony leather-cased agenda, and the air filled with his arrogance, separated us. I settled in and called home but was distracted by his smirk and recurrent unwelcomed glare. Not remembering the country code, I was unable to provide my family with my new complete French mobile phone number. My supposed inefficiency bothered him. His annoyed, purposeful chuckle reverberated in my ear. I gathered my belongings and changed seats, leaving him alone with his pompous attitude and desired privacy. The woman who had occasionally looked up at us from across the aisle now remained completely absorbed in her book. Through the corner of slim haute couture glasses, a strikingly chic man caught me admiring his calfskin shoes. I averted my glance to avoid further embarrassment.

As we pulled into the station, I felt sentimental seeing the Basilica of Lisieux on-top-of the hill. I couldn't help but think that even if I lived here, I would never tire of its awe-inspiring view. Since it was already late in the afternoon, I decided I would visit the basilica the following day.

Without a map, I explored the town for a few hours before heading to Cathédrale Sainte-Pierre, which was only forty metres from my hotel and, therefore, a logical place to visit before nightfall. As I walked slowly down the nave towards the high altar Saint Thérèse's father donated, I stared agape, admiring the Gothic arches and large pillars. The darkening sky could be seen through the stained-glass windows, adding an extra layer of cold to the church. The only sounds came from a gentleman who passed by me. The wheels of his carry-on rattled and scraped the stone floor and his footsteps echoed as he rushed through the church. He appeared to be making a last-minute stop before leaving Lisieux.

I lit three candles, knelt, and prayed. I then sat in front of a circular stand with varying sizes of haphazardly positioned candles. Many of them had melted wax that had dripped and hardened along their sides. The glow and movement of the flickering flames almost lulled me to sleep so I decided it best to get some fresh air and grab a bite to eat.

After enjoying a savoury crêpe topped with fresh fruit and ice cream, I returned to my hotel. The light rain had stopped and most of the clouds had cleared. Once I was settled in my room, I opened the windows and leaned out to look at the twilight sky and few distant stars before closing the shutters. I didn't expect to hear birds chirping as though it were dawn.

I welcomed my first day in Lisieux, and all the days thereafter, by opening the tall, narrow windows and weathered wooden shutters. Letting both the morning and evening air of Normandy flow into my room and hearing the birds sing was a distinct pleasure. They sang sweet melodies l hadn't heard before. The sheer white drapes seemed to gently flutter in harmony to their song.

There was an abundance of roses in bloom throughout the town and they appeared strong and healthy from growing in rich soil. The idea of fertile land reminded me of Saint Thérèse's words in her memoir, *The Story of a Soul*, where she recounts to her father:

> I sat down beside him, not saying a word, but there were tears in my eyes. ... "What is it, Little Queen? Tell me." ... I told him about Carmel and my longing to enter soon, and then he too began to weep, but never said a word against my vocation, only that I was still rather young to make such a serious decision. When I insisted and gave him all my reasons, his ... heart was soon convinced. ... Going to a low stone wall, he showed me some little white flowers, ... he picked one of them and gave it to me, explaining how carefully God had brought it to blossom and preserved it till that day. So striking was the resemblance between the little flower and little Thérèse that it seemed as if I were listening to the story of my own life. I took the flower as if it were some relic, noticing that when Father had tried to pluck it, the roots had come out too, ... as though destined to start life again in some other and more fertile soil. Father

was doing just the same for me, letting me be transplanted to Mount Carmel ... .[12]

---

[12]   Thérèse, *The Story of a Soul,* 74.

Ask the Lord of the harvest,
therefore, to send out workers
into his harvest field.

Matthew 9:38

In Town

Since I visited the monastery, basilica, cemetery, and her family home several times, I can't begin to put order to the discoveries made at these places. I didn't write a journal; instead, I preferred to capture images that spoke volumes to my soul. Given that I can't help but see beauty in the mundane, I averaged about 250 pictures a day. I was attracted to antique door knockers patinated perfectly by the air and rain, which begged to be tapped; by the appeal of a typical blue shutter of Normandy—painted, yet flaked by the seasons, and slightly opened in the mid-afternoon; by the way fresh artichokes for sale were positioned in overused wooden crates on a street corner; by how artisan bread was strategically displayed so that the light of the crystal chandelier refracted off the mirror to shine on its perfect crust; and by how the queue of people to enter such a bakery continued outside. These occurrences of everyday French life grabbed me. Then beckoned the glorious colourful mosaics in the basilica, waiting to be immortalized further by my snapshot, as did the extravagant Norman mansions, each one unique in its design and beauty that adorned the seaside of Trouville-Deauville. I was so comfortable and at ease in France, to the point where I dare say that when I walked through the streets of Lisieux, it felt as if I had lived there before.

As I have no definite recollection of the sequence of events that unfolded during my sojourn, I must describe them inconsecutively. Perhaps it is now most fitting to write in this manner, considering it's the spontaneous fashion in which Saint Thérèse expressed herself in her autobiography.

I cherished being in her home, experienced a singular event at mass, and received a rare request at the cemetery. I was overwhelmed at the Carmel. I didn't have grand expectations about visiting the Carmelite monastery, yet it's where I was most profoundly affected. My heart was seized. I prayed, meditated, and contemplated in front of the Virgin Statue of Smiles, situated high above her relics, while listening to the solemn choir that resounded like a symphony of angels. With unending amazement, I read every one of the plaques inscribed with written words of gratitude through the blurriness of my tear-filled eyes. I was eager to see the exact spot where a picture of Saint Thérèse lying on a bed was taken one month before she departed for her eternal life. This image of her under the arch saddens me every time I look at it. She's resting on fresh-looking linens, propped up by many large pillows; however, the woollen blankets that covered her appear heavy, scratchy, and uncomfortable. She was brought "outside under the cloister on a rolling bed, as far as the open door of the choir, for her last visit to the Blessed Sacrament. Before bringing her back to the infirmary, Sister Genevieve photographed her dropping rose petals on her crucifix."[13] A few weeks prior to her death, Saint Thérèse repeated this act and prophetically advised, "Collect these petals, my little sisters, they will help you do favours later on ... Don't lose any of them."[13] Miracles were attributed to those who had access to these petals after her passing. Saint Thérèse had suffered in agony. After a drawn-out battle with tuberculosis, which had damaged all but half of one lung, she took her last breath on the 30th of September 1897.

I was kindly welcomed at the hermitage. Looking through the large glass foyer doors, I saw beautiful roses and a statue of Saint Thérèse straightaway. I entered the courtyard and took pictures, all the while peeking at her statue. I heard a soft voice whisper in my heart: *Come ... come sit on my lap!* Immediately, I dismissed this call yet felt guilty in doing so; it just seemed such an odd invitation to hear. I continued to snap a few more photos before I drifted towards her monument. Hesitantly and reluctantly, I questioned her on my way: *What did you just say? I can't sit on your lap. I don't fit.* I couldn't seem to grasp the intended meaning of her call or my equally strange response.

I stood in front of the statue and reached inside my purse. I carried two of my children's small stuffed animals with me as a reminder of them. In turn, they were happy to have their favourite bunnies travel with me across the ocean to a special place where I would ask for them to be blessed. For a moment, I wondered

---

[13]   Pierre Descouvemont and Helmuth Nils Loose, *Therese and Lisieux*, trans. Salvatore Sciurba and Louis Pambrun, (Toronto: Novalis, 1996), 299.

where I should put them while I prayed. Then, instinctively, I placed them in the cradle of Saint Thérèse's folded hands. At that moment, I realized she wasn't asking me to sit on her lap! I was amused; endearingly, she had called the bunnies. Snuggled together, they fit perfectly on her lap. Instantly, I remembered the words she quoted from scripture: "Whosoever is a little one, let him come to Me (Prov. 9:4)."[14]

---

[14]   Thérèse, *The Story of a Soul*, 140.

And now these three remain:
faith, hope and love.
But the greatest of these is love.

1 Corinthians 13:13

The Carmel

The Carmel is situated a few steps away from the hermitage, just past the banks of the Orbiquet River. Outside, in front of the entry doors, stands a statue of Saint Thérèse. In movies, I had seen devotees vigorously rub pieces of cloth on relics, hoping for blessings to be bestowed on them. Prompted by these images, I brought some hankies to sweep on significant objects, wishing for the same. I wiped them on the cheeks of the statue and with purpose I prayed. I requested that one day she stand before the throne of God on behalf of whoever will hold these pieces of fabric and help dry their tears while assisting them in their difficulties. I beseeched her with confidence. I finished my last supplication and closed my eyes in prayer. An exceptional moment ensued.

Suddenly, a swift wind swooshed around me. I stood in the middle of this swirling band of air. Caught by further surprise, I smelled a distinct perfume of roses, which grew increasingly stronger as I began to sense the presence of blossoms floating within this rapid air stream. Upon opening my eyes, the flurry then faded, and the scent dissipated all too quickly. I was amazed by these wondrous signs since there wasn't a breeze that entire day and the only flowers nearby were those across the distant pathway, behind the brick and glass of the convent walls. Through this mysterious event, Saint Thérèse had confirmed that she was with me, and my requests had been heard. With veneration and contemplation, I slowly folded each piece of cloth, guarding them as more valuable than precious jewels and glittering gold.

It's difficult for me to put into words the depth of my emotions whenever I visited the Carmel. I knelt in front of her reliquary and especially loved to do so when the Carmelites sang. A sign informs visitors that "the largest parts of Saint Thérèse's relics are enclosed in a casket underneath the statue that represents her on her deathbed." On the walls and alongside the black iron gate that encloses the reliquary are stone plaques engraved with words of thankfulness for graces, healings, and miracles received. Out of need for inspiration, and longing to acknowledge and bear witness to their claims, I read each one of these testimonies of God's enduring love and limitless power. I cried a sea of tears. In another room, an entire wall is dedicated to other such affirmations. Tokens, beautiful trinkets, valued personal items, and hand-carved wooden objects are displayed inside glass casings. I was surrounded by proclamations of faith and favours received. The rooms are an oasis of hope and love.

Also showcased are four swords, a brass and a copper bullet—both undamaged—fragments of ammunition, and unique vintage World War I medals of valour from soldiers whose lives were healed or spared through Saint Thérèse's intercession. I wondered about the hidden stories behind these once merciless swords, the intact and exploded bullet pieces, and the badges of honour donated in recognition of her intervention.

Documented cards on display recount how in 1914 French soldiers reported seeing apparitions of Saint Thérèse in various battlefields. "She emerged at times holding a cross, other times a sabre. She spoke to them, calmed their fears, resolved their doubts, and helped them overcome temptation. A heroine to the soldiers, she consoled and protected them. She appeared to them in their dreams." They referred to her as "my war patroness," "the angel of battles," "the shield of soldiers," "my dear little Captain," "my second guardian angel," and "my little sister of the trenches." Medals and prayer cards of Saint Thérèse miraculously stopped rifle bullets like "real shields," saving the lives of the soldiers who carried them. I was fascinated by the description written on another information card: "Planes and artillery pieces were named after her. Entire regiments were consecrated to her. She had an astounding effect on the combatants. Two thousand two hundred stories about Saint Thérèse of the Child Jesus' intercession, exclusive to wartime soldiers, were recorded in a separate fourth part edition of Volume V of *Pluie de Roses*."

Framed international newspaper clippings and two boxes filled with letters from all four corners of the world attest to how believers were saved through her aid. Through the glass lids of these wooden-framed boxes, I looked closely at the stamps on the envelopes. I was intrigued by these concealed letters from Malta,

Brazil, Russia, Poland, Belgium, Holland, Thailand, Italy, Syria, Rwanda, Austria, Lebanon, the Philippines, Saint Lucia, Bulgaria, Columbia, Tanganyika, Yugoslavia, the Republic of Cameroon, the United States of America, and countries whose names I could not decipher.

My heart was arrested with inexplicable emotion. I copied down the words written on the inscription that was placed inside one of the boxes. It read: "Saint Thérèse is close to all in distress. We regularly hear about her intervention in physical healing (spectacular) as well as in thousands of different miracles within circles of family, friends, or, of professional people." I folded and tucked away this small piece of paper deep into my cargo pants side pocket; over time, it became softened and wrinkled.

I used to love growing flowers,
and making little altars too,
in a niche which I had been lucky enough
to find in the garden wall.

Saint Thérèse

Les Buissonets

The following account is not a dream, but it felt like one. My heart raced as I walked down the cobblestone road leading up to 22 *Chemin des Buissonets.* The three-floor Martin family home is hidden behind a stone wall that runs the length of the property. I slightly opened the wooden door that grants access from the road to their front lawn, peeked inside, and then entered. Roses beautified the grounds. Under a cloudless, pale blue sky, I freely and serenely lingered on the pebble-stone pathway that led from the street entrance doorway to the front door of her home. Saint Thérèse lived in this house with her father, Louis, and her four sisters. They had moved there from Alençon after their mother,

Zélie, had died. The girls called their new home, *Les Buissonets* (*The Little Bushes*).

Once inside, I thought of how Saint Thérèse, as a young child, pranced around on the very same burnt-orange and grey tiled floor on which I stood. My mind wandered, and I remembered other places where she had once been. I recalled a scene from her autobiography where she passionately describes her pilgrimage in Rome. I envisioned her running recklessly on the ground in the Coliseum:

> Here ... I was seeing with my own eyes that arena where so many martyrs had shed their blood for Jesus, and I wanted to stoop and kiss the soil, which their glorious trials had sanctified. What a disappointment! The ground had been raised and the real arena was buried. ... No one dared go in among such dangerous ruins. Yet could one possibly be in Rome and not go down? It was impossible, and from then on, I did not take any notice of what the guide was saying. ... I said to Céline: "Follow me, ..." We both ran forward at once, scrambling over the ruins, which crumbled under our feet, while Father shouted after us, astonished. But we did not hear. As warriors of old felt their courage grow in the face of danger, so our joy increased ... I pressed my lips to the dust once reddened with the blood of the early

Christians, and I asked the grace to be a martyr too for Jesus. [15]

Seeing the hearth where Saint Thérèse used to place her slippers on Christmas Eve reminded me of the story of when she and her family returned home after attending midnight mass. While she was going up the stairs, she overheard her father express an unusual sentiment of "annoyance"[16] to her sister for having to fill the slippers with presents, hoping that it would "be the last year."[16] Sensitive as Saint Thérèse was, she didn't cry upon hearing his words, but, instead, ran down the stairs and opened her gifts happily. Realizing that she had been privy to their conversation, they were quite surprised and relieved by her reaction. As I ascended the stairs, I pictured the then thirteen-year-old Thérèse descending them that Christmas morning—the day she claims she received "the grace of [her] complete conversion,"[16] when she was finally able to put the feelings of others above her own.

Many of her childhood treasures are displayed behind a glass wall: her atlas, blocks, skipping rope, history books, communion dress, and the cross she prayed to when she saved her first soul, the criminal Pranzini. I looked out her bedroom window facing the front lawn and imagined how she had done the same. I walked through their house and the grounds and meditated in the backyard garden.

---

[15]   Thérèse, *The Story of a Soul*, 92, 93.

[16]   Thérèse, *Story of a Soul*, third edition, 98.

They asked each other,
"Were not our hearts burning within us
while he talked with us on the road
and opened the Scriptures to us?"

Luke 24:32

The Basilica

The local clergy opposed the idea of constructing a basilica in honour of Saint Thérèse.[17] Pope Pius XI didn't agree with their rationale that interest in her had reached its peak. He asked the bishop of Bayeux, Monsignor Suhard, that the building be "very large, very beautiful and completed as quickly as possible."[17] The basilica, which can seat 4,000 people, boasts colourful mosaics, stained-glass windows, a thirty-seven-metre-high vaulted ceiling, and an extraordinary dome. A brightly lit Art Deco crypt lies beneath the basilica and is adorned with lustrous gold-tiled

---

17   Descouvemont and Loose, *Therese and Lisieux*, 324.

mosaics. Many transparent plaques inscribed with white Theresian quotes are situated inside arched chapels that line the length of the left sidewall of the basilica. Substantial posters of Saint Thérèse, some in sepia tones, decorate the walls.

An enormous poster depicting Saint Thérèse with Saint Théophane Venard was temporarily on display as was a relic of his. A framed information plaque describes the connection between these two saints. He was a French priest and missionary who desired martyrdom from the age of nine. At thirty-one, his wish came true in Hanoi, Tonkin, a place known for beheading Christians. Saint Thérèse, desiring to be a missionary and evangelist, wanted to move to Saigon to live in the Carmelite monastery. Her superiors explained that the region would not be a suitable place due to her poor health. Wanting to also be a martyr, she set her hopes on going to the Carmel in Hanoi, but, again, wasn't granted permission. For these and other reasons, Saint Thérèse felt that her spirituality was closely akin to his.[18]

At the basilica, I attended one of the most meaningful masses of my life. An impressive number of priests were in attendance. I wondered why so many had assembled on that Sunday. Never had I seen a church filled with so many clergymen. I imagined they spoke various languages and were of different nationalities. I counted thirty of them as they walked towards the sacristy doors, and I didn't even count all of them. There was a continuous stream of flowing white robes. The bottom of their albs flapped as they strode by.

---

[18]   Information plaque entitled: Soeur Thérèse et Théophane Vénard: Missions Étrangères, 350 ans d'histoire et d'aventure en Asie, n.d. Displayed at the Basilica of Lisieux.

During mass, and for the first time, I understood the real significance of the Eucharist. The priest devoted half an hour to the preparation of the blessing of the bread and wine. With adoration, he solemnly lifted the Host upward towards Heaven, in the slowest motion I'd ever seen or thought possible. The wafer was astonishingly huge; it completely covered the view of his face. Never had I witnessed a moment such as the one when he honoured the Eucharist in a profoundly sacred way, demonstrating his belief that it is truly The Living Christ. I presumed the sacrament of Holy Communion was always celebrated this way at the basilica. About a thousand or more souls were focused on the altar. When the celebrant lowered the Host, everyone bowed their head in unison. All these movements were perfectly orchestrated. The reverence shown was extraordinary. You could hear a pin drop.

But those who hope in the Lord will renew their strength.
They will soar on wings like eagles;
they will run and not grow weary,
they will walk and not be faint.

Isaiah 40:31a

The Cemetery

Slowly, I ascended the inclined road to the left of the basilica, the same route one takes towards Paris. I was unsure of the distance to the cemetery or how long it would take for me to arrive. I saw a sign and simply followed its direction. My legs grew tired earlier than I had thought they would. Along the way, my condition forced me to rest for a short while on a street-side bench. I welcomed the drizzling rain. I just hoped I wouldn't be caught in an unexpected downpour; this had happened to me already during my second afternoon in Lisieux while walking down this same sloped road from the basilica. Places were closed on Sundays, so I couldn't browse in a boutique or enter a pastry shop for a warm cocoa and dessert until the rain subsided. I had no choice but to continue my promenade, and I decided to do so in a carefree spirit. If anyone had peered through a window to look at the stormy weather and happened to see me, they might have asked themselves what I could have possibly been smiling about as I walked alone on a deserted street in the rain. Suddenly, Heaven's water cascaded upon me, instantly matting my hair to my face. I looked down at my pants; they were sopping and sagging. My feet were submerged in flowing water. If it weren't for the view of my flip-flop straps, one would have thought I was walking barefoot through the sea.

Completely drenched, I searched for a covered doorway to take refuge. Finally, I caught a glimpse of a single step under an open archway. I quickly leapt towards it. Unexpectedly, I found myself standing directly underneath an umbrella held by a young man who was caught by the same surprise. I looked up at him and was at a loss for words; he, however, was not. We were on a narrow pathway that was protected by high stone walls and a partial roof, which shielded us from the storm. The rain dripped down the sides of his black umbrella, trickling to the ground. Behind us was a fenced-in rectangular courtyard garden. The late spring blossoms were meticulously groomed. The sunrays peeked through the monochrome grey sky, casting a spotlight over these orange blooms, while the pathway where we stood remained dark. To the left of us was an old, hidden, peculiar stone stairway. It had an exotic and intriguing appeal, like one that might be found in a faraway land. The stranger proposed that we go up the spiral stairs to his place for a cup of Moroccan tea. Naturally, I declined his offer. Instead, I briefly admired this secluded place and then turned and walked back a few steps towards the entrance from which I'd come. I looked at and listened to the pouring rain as it rhythmically beat the pavement, waiting for its diminuendo so that I could venture on.

En route to the cemetery, I knew there would be no such shelter. With an anxious and longing heart, I dared to find it despite the changing temperamental sky. I looked over my shoulder to gauge the distance that I had walked. I realized that I hadn't travelled far since the basilica was still close behind. More than an ideal postcard snapshot, the backdrop was a perfect *tableau*.

As I walked up the hill, I thought of the first pilgrims who made their way to Saint Thérèse's gravesite. Earnestly, I continued onwards. Once I arrived at the cemetery, I eagerly looked for signage indicating the way to her burial site. I did not find one. I turned left, walked straight ahead, and descended several steps. I was captivated as I walked by the tombs; they were extremely old and decrepit. One of them caused me to take great pause. A few yellow-flowered weeds erupted through the pebbles, creating an appealing contrast to the charcoal-coloured stone slab. Through time, the tombstone had lifted, along with its supporting foundation. A large, heavy, rusted chain, attached to twelve solid iron stands, surrounded this large, pitted sepulchre that was sparsely covered with moss. Each tilted column had shifted considerably, likely to never again be repositioned properly. I wondered when the last friend or relative might have visited this person's burial site.

The mausoleums resembled small chapels. Although I had seen larger-than-life statues representing a deceased farmer and his animals in a cemetery in Turin, Italy, these chapels were unique and engaging in a completely different way. I was mesmerized. Lured, I entered a few of them by squeezing myself in sideways.

I dismissed any terrifying thought of getting locked inside one because the ornate iron gates were jammed into partially opened positions. I noticed that in this section of the cemetery, many of the buried souls were born in the middle of the nineteenth century. Within these chapels, I found pewter crucifixes affixed on either teal blue or red velvet crosses, confirming that the ones I acquired at an antique shop in Trouville were authentic and from the Napoleon III era. I contemplated whether I should pick up the fallen crosses and respectfully place them on their original hooks or leave them, as history should have it, on the tiled floor covered in dirt, cobwebs, twigs, dried leaves, and rumpled paper that had been blown inside by the wind. I carefully lifted one of them out of the debris and turned it over to look at its backside. The material had become so fragile over the years that it disintegrated upon barely touching it, like when a charred piece of paper is handled and crumbles to ashes.

One family had a tall monument that reigned from on High. Its beauty and intricate design hypnotized me. It pleaded for and demanded my attention. I pondered the identities of these deceased souls and how wealthy they must have been to have afforded such a mausoleum. In contrast, I would soon discover the simplest of crosses where an actual saint had once been laid to rest.

The white sky, scattered with hints of platinum grey, showed promise of rain. I marched down a few more steps. Below, to my right, I spotted the backside of Saint Thérèse's statue and gravesite overlooking the rolling hills of Normandy. From this view, it appeared as though she was watching over and protecting her homeland. No one was at the cemetery. Stillness filled the air. Humbled by the reality that this awaited occasion would begin to unfold, I slowly, and without a sound, opened the low-lying, slightly rusted, ivory gate in front of the Carmelite's plot. Breaking the silence, the church bells promptly announced my arrival. Through the harmonious chiming melody, I perceived the faint crunching sound of my footsteps on the grey, white, and amber-coloured stones.

I tried to imagine how very few people were in attendance for her burial in the fall of 1897, while contemplating how "500,000 faithful"[19] would later attend her canonization in Rome in the spring of 1925. The original white wooden cross that marked Saint Thérèse's first gravesite was enclosed in a larger one made of glass and stone. At the base, between these two crosses, lay a heap of ashes. A few faded, rolled scrolls jetted out from this pile; some were slightly scorched along their edges. I presumed they were displayed to represent the other handwritten notes that were reduced to cinder. Maybe there wouldn't have been enough room to store all the letters had some not been burned. I was curious about these notes. *Who wrote them? Were they messages of gratitude? Requests for intercession? Had the notes been placed there on September 6, 1910, after Saint Thérèse's remains were exhumed?* I wondered about the events that transpired that day and on March 23, 1923, when she was solemnly carried to her reliquary at the Carmel. I wiped some cloths on the glass pane that shielded the preserved cross. On my knees, I prayed, silently fulfilling the act I had once dreamt of performing. I sat before her statue and pondered her life and mine.

During one of my visits to the cemetery, I prayed for a sign. I craved one even though I had received many of them.

---

[19]   Descouvemont and Loose, *Therese and Lisieux*, 322.

Upon preparing to leave her burial site, I heard a guiding voice within me. This time, I didn't question what I heard. Instead, I immediately listened and followed the instructions given. With exactitude, I was directed to pick the petals off a rose, from one of the rose bushes near her statue. The flower was covered in dew. The symbolism of water and life came to mind. The voice conveyed to my heart, *put the water on your legs!* I picked two petals shimmering in dewdrops but explained to my Little Flower that there was not nearly enough water on them. Faithfully, however, I obeyed. I sat down, rolled up my jeans, dampened my legs with a few droplets, and waited to see if my twisted, enlarged varicose veins would be healed instantaneously. Nothing happened. I tiptoed towards the rosebush, gently reminding her on my way that there wasn't sufficient water on the petals. Hoping to find more dewdrops, I selected another petal. Carefully, I peeled it back from the flower, which had not yet fully bloomed. I was amazed. The base of this delicate petal was brimming with water. It looked like a ladle! I couldn't believe my eyes! I was quite unsure how to remove this tiny yellow cup filled with water without spilling a precious drop.

I thought about some of the miracles that had occurred here at Saint Thérèse's tomb site. I wondered if this water would be my source of new life. Steadily, I carried the petal to a place where I could sit inconspicuously should someone happen to pass by. I spread the refreshingly cool water on my legs and made the sign of the cross on my forehead with what ended up being the last drop. Not to lose these three fragrant petals, I tucked them into my pocket. I returned to the rose and opened every petal in search of more of this mysterious water. Each remaining petal was completely dry. I was thankful for the unusual experience even though I didn't receive a miraculous cure. The petals from the rose, nourished in sacred soil, became a token of Saint Thérèse's undying love for me. Soundlessly, I closed the gate behind me. The bells then mystically tolled my farewell, as they had my arrival.

.

Dear God, You alone know all that I endured!

Saint Thérèse

Love

One nun made the following comment about Saint Thérèse: "She is very good, but she has certainly never done anything worth speaking about."[20] Saint Thérèse kept her sacrifices hidden from those with whom she lived. During her life, she saw herself as little, like "the obscure grain of sand trampled underfoot by passers-by."[21] Pope Pius X viewed her differently. After her death, in 1914, "he had told a missionary bishop privately that Sister Thérèse was 'the greatest saint of modern times.'"[22] His description of her proved prophetic.

---

[20]   Thérèse, *The Story of a Soul*, 210.

[21]   Thérèse, *Story of a Soul*, third edition, 207.

[22]   Ibid., 287.

I was fascinated by how a cloistered Carmelite nun, who lived an ordinary life in a small northern French town, could attain such acclaim! Under obedience, Saint Thérèse was directed to recount the story of her childhood. She completed her assignment in three separate sections, addressed to three people, over a three-year period. Closer to her death, she was asked to add her reflections on religious life, which became the final part of her manuscript. Months before her passing, Saint Thérèse had a feeling that her writings would serve as part of her posthumous mission and knew that it would be published. Her compilations, which were not originally intended for publication, became her autobiography, *Histoire d'une Ame (Story of a Soul)*. On the one-year anniversary of her death, 2,000 copies of her book were printed.[23] Her memoir, now considered to be a spiritual classic, has been translated into more than sixty languages—an indication of her worldwide popularity.

Saint Thérèse had a strong desire to love God and win Him souls. She spoke these words to Jesus:

> I long to bring light to souls, like the prophets and doctors; to go to the ends of the earth to preach Your name, to plant Your glorious Cross … on pagan shores. … Open the Book of life, my Jesus; see all the deeds recorded of the Saints! All these I want to perform for You! What can You say in the face of all this foolishness of mine, for surely I am the littlest and the weakest soul on earth? … Perhaps my vast desires are only a

---

23   Ibid., xiv-xix.

dream and nothing but folly? If this is so, I beg You to make it clear to me. ... If my desires are overly bold, then take them away, because they are my greatest martyrdom.[24]

Sister Marie of the Sacred Heart asked Saint Thérèse to share the secrets that Jesus confided to her. She reveals: "I understood [that love comprised all vocations, that love was everything, that it embraced all times and places, ... in a word, that it was eternal!]"[25]

Her aspirations won my heart. I am renewed by her love. Her wisdom enlightens me. Saint Thérèse composed plays, poems, letters, prayers, and the following most beautiful parable to explain God's foreseeing love and mercy:

Suppose a clever physician's child meets with a stone in his path, which causes him to fall and break a limb. His father comes to him immediately, picks him up lovingly, takes care of this hurt, using all the resources of his profession for this. His child, completely cured, shows his gratitude. This child is no doubt right in loving his father! But I am going to make another comparison. The father knowing there is a stone in his child's way hastens ahead of him and removes it but without anyone's seeing him do it. Certainly, this child, the object of his father's tender foresight, but UNAWARE of the misfortune from which he

---

24   Thérèse, *The Story of a Soul*, 197, 198, 203.

25   Thérèse, *Story of a Soul*, third edition, 194.

was delivered by him, will not thank him and *will love him less* than if he had been cured by him. But if he should come to learn the danger from which he escaped, *will he not love his father more?* Well, I am this child, the object of the foreseeing love of a Father who has not sent His Word to save the just, but sinners.[26]

---

[26]   Ibid., 84.

*The Spirit intercedes for the saints
in accordance with God's will.*

Romans 8:27

Journeys

About two years prior to my trip to Lisieux, a seed of faith had been planted in my soul without my awareness. Later, I understood that this new source of life needed years of nourishment to grow. The depth and width of my faith had to expand; I had to experience interior suffering, mingled with a tempestuous ocean of tears before this grain could flourish.

"Lourdes," the first chapter of my spiritual memoir, was completed a year-and-a-half after I visited this southwestern French town. My recollection of the marvellous event that transpired at the Massabielle Grotto remains as vivid as when it first happened.

After I returned home from my second trip to Italy, I tried to continue journaling but was incapable of composing any just phrase about my stay in the Eternal City. For a year, I was confronted with nothing but failed efforts. My pursuit to express myself became insurmountable. Full of anguish and concealed emotion, I was completely blocked from writing successfully. I then met the exceptional Saint Thérèse. With her in my life, the melancholy in my heart and soul began to lift. As the seasons changed, so did I. During the autumn months that followed our initial encounter, I attempted to write again. To my delight, the words began to flow effortlessly, like a zephyr.

Two years had elapsed between my trips to Rome and Lisieux. I left Normandy with well over a thousand pictures and a diary of unwritten sentiments cached in my heart. I often thought about the letters stored in the glass-encased wooden boxes exhibited at the Carmel. *Who wrote them and what graces did they receive through Saint Thérèse's intercession?* I could never have fathomed the significance of the paper upon which I had copied down the inscription, along with the names of the countries imprinted on the stamps. A highly unusual occurrence took place regarding this paper; but, before I describe this event, I must first share my thoughts, which are drawn back to an inspirational passage written by Saint Thérèse.

She describes a two-month pilgrimage she took with her father, Louis, and her sister, Céline. Before reaching the Eternal City, their destination, they travelled through Switzerland, with "its towering mountains, whose snow-capped peaks were lost in the clouds, with its waterfalls and its deep valleys, rich with giant ferns and purple heather."[27] She characterizes herein her travels:

---

[27]   Thérèse, *The Story of a Soul*, 87.

... we were ... by a broad lake with calm, clear waters mingling their azure with the crimson of the setting sun. I cannot say what an impression the magnificence and grandeur of these scenes made upon me. ... Then I thought of the religious life as it really is, with its restrictions and its little hidden sacrifices every day. ... I thought to myself: "Later on, in the hour of trial, when enclosed in Carmel, I shall only be able to see a little corner of the sky; I will look back on today and be encouraged; the thought of God's majesty and greatness will put my own small troubles in their place. ... ."[28]

On this trip, they visited Paris, Milan, Venice, Padua, Bologna, Loreto, Rome, Naples, Pompeii, Pisa, and Florence. I contemplate how she gave up all opportunity to ever travel and see the world again by entering the monastery. I imagine her there, at the Carmel, perhaps looking up at a *small corner of blue sky*.

Then, I marvel even further at how, from living an obscure life in a cloistered convent, she would be able to reach millions of people worldwide after her death. Thousands of people would write letters to the monastery in Lisieux, affirming accounts of graces and miracles received through her intercession. In July 1914, the Carmel had received an astonishing average of 200 letters a day; 512 on the 9th of February 1918; and ultimately culminating in a daily average of 800-1,000 in April 1923.[29] The

---

[28]   Ibid., 87, 88.

[29]   Thérèse, Story of a Soul, third edition, 287.

envelopes on display at the Carmel came from all corners of the earth. Thinking of them, with their protected testimonies inside, did an abundance of good for my soul.

Fate is not the Ruler,
but the servant of Providence.

Baron Edward G. Bulwer-Lytton

26 November 2009

I will now explain the details behind the *highly unusual occurrence* that I referenced earlier. The thought of it being a mere coincidence would simply shatter the truth.

The mid-afternoon air felt more brisk than usual for most end-of-November days. The azure sky was dotted with fluffy clouds, and the sun added a touch of warmth to the chilled air. Most of the leaves had already fallen and been raked; some remained on the maple tree, and a few had fluttered down onto me while I was positioning Christmas reindeer decorations. In the holiday spirit, I dressed up the globe-shaped bushes with mini lights. Partially satisfied with my unfinished display, I went inside to prepare an aromatic cider drink.

Later that evening, when our family gathered at the dinner table to eat, I found a piece of paper partially tucked under my dish that I had set earlier. I asked my children where it came from and who had put it there. No one answered. I turned it over; the words *Hôtel de la Place* jumped off the page. Immediately, I recognized this as the backside of the paper on which I had copied the inscription about Saint Thérèse's intercession, along with the names of the countries from where the letters originated—the letters showcased at the Carmel that I desperately wanted to read. Bewildered, I asked myself how this piece of paper from Lisieux could have reappeared. And why on this particular day?

My husband had found it under the tree in the front yard, resting beneath the gem boxwood bush I had covered in lights earlier in the day. I didn't notice it or its starkness against the graphite slate landscape stones. Oddly enough, he spotted it and bothered to bring it inside rather than simply throw it away. He had no knowledge of its origin. I tried to make sense of how the paper showed up in our yard. It couldn't have fallen out of my pocket because I was wearing winter clothing and not the spring attire I'd worn when I was in Lisieux. More thoughts swirled around in my mind. It was the end of fall and I had used the leaf blower many times. The lawn had been mowed and raked often. I wondered how this strip of paper could lie undisturbed on the ground. *Why was it not blown away by the wind, picked up with the fallen leaves, or seen earlier by my attentive eyes?*

Six and a half months had gone by since my return from France. This forgotten piece of paper had now suddenly and mysteriously resurfaced. Stored in a sturdy, sealed folder, it had been placed on a high shelf in the entrance closet—along with my other mementoes from Lisieux. I tried to comprehend how it had emerged but knew such an attempt would be futile. With utmost certainty, I say to you, Saint Thérèse was speaking to me on that end-of-November day.

When I held the paper, I sensed she was communicating with me. I interpreted its mystical reappearance as a prophetic sign. I felt her spirit and presence. I had a strong suspicion that she was letting me know that an important handwritten letter I had sent to Lisieux had arrived!

Re-reading the inscription reminded me of the many items displayed at the Carmel. Just knowing of the existence of the swords, plaques, and trinkets was a powerful source of inspiration. From the moment I saw the envelopes in the box, my heart ached to read the letters they concealed. So great was my desire that I contacted a certain monsignor at the basilica in Lisieux. I knew all too well that my request to be granted permission to read them was a bold one. I'd been awaiting his response for a few months. My enormous yearning had evolved into an unexpected desire not only to read them but to share them with others so that they too could feel renewed with hope.

There is more to this anecdote. During my outings in Lisieux, I had purchased a few crucifixes from the Napoleon III era. I didn't think I needed another one until the day before my departure home. While treasure-hunting at an outdoor flea market, I'd seen one buried halfway down a cardboard box. After leaving the marketplace, I regretted not having bought it. I longed for it and flew through the streets in search of the market. All the streets began to look the same. I was lost and couldn't find my way back to the town square that I'd happened upon earlier. When I asked some passersby for directions, they reacted as though it didn't exist. The whole scenario in which I found myself made me desire that crucifix even more. The pewter crucifix was adhered to a discoloured red crushed-velvet cross and a third of the price I had paid in Trouville. Frantically, I ran through the streets in search of the antique dealers. Finally, in the distance, I spotted the large, aged oak tree under which three nonchalant, charming Frenchmen had previously sat, selling their artifacts. I was disheartened; they were gone, along with their worn-out boxes and my prized cross. I puttered over the earth and acorns, slightly dusting my feet in dirt.

Disappointed, I lingered around, hoping to find something else to buy to fill my displeasure of being left empty-handed. I loved the old pharmacy flask that was pasty white inside, etched with the deposits of calcium. I learned the reason behind this chalky residue from the wavy, tousle-haired man whom I'd previously met at the market—but he, too, was gone. As he described the process of how the glass acquired its appeal, I remained mesmerized. Captivatingly, he explained that pharmacists were real chemists back then as he swirled his hand in a manner like he was holding some ancient stirring rod. Spellbound, I could envision a room and a pharmacist from a bygone era. I wondered, *who is this man with stylishly disheveled, shoulder-length hair, dressed in seemingly worn clothes, that speaks like this?* His humour, knowledge, and simplicity enchanted me. I thought to myself, *he should be a screenwriter.*

Charmed, it seemed fitting to speak poetry back to him, in French, of course. He continued to speak fascinatingly about the other few items he was selling, such as the old elementary school coat hooks. Oh, how I'd have loved to bring them home to use in our mudroom! I would've liked to hear more from this creative soul, but there were more stands to inspect under the soon to be setting sun.

Only a few people remained milling about the market. Dealers were slowly packing up their antiques. The atmosphere was quiet, almost melancholic. Dusk rays diffused through a hanging, hollow, olive-green glass ball. I took it off the hook and held it fastidiously in my hand. This fabulous *boule* entwined in a golden-brown, slightly frayed netted rope, was once used to attach to a fisherman's net in order to identify its location in the sea. I knew it dated from around the 1930s or 1940s since I had also bought one of them in delightful Trouville. Slowly, I studied it for cracks and imperfections, all the while thinking of where I would put it on display in my home. More importantly, I was taking into account how it would fit in my already overstuffed suitcase. Out of the corner of my eye, I noticed a couple closely watching me. I wondered why. *Perhaps I looked like a fortune-teller gazing into a crystal ball.*

The locals made their way towards me. The woman intentionally stood next to me and looked at the glass fishing float I was carefully holding. She began to speak to me, mentioning how her friend had asked her only a few weeks before if she wanted some of these same types of glass *boules*. Not knowing what to do with them, she had refused the offer. She motioned to the size of a large, overflowing box as she explained that her friend, feeling the same, simply disposed of them. My heart sank. I thought, *oh, they could have filled an empty valise and made such charming gifts from the French seaside!* I imagined the antique market dealers would've loved to have had them, too. I consoled myself: one day I would return to France with an extra suitcase, just for market-found treasures.

She then looked at me with an inspired smile, remembering that she might have one stashed away somewhere in her house—she just wasn't quite sure where. When she heard the asking price, which was again far less than what I'd paid in Trouville, she emphatically whispered, "*Non ... mais non!*" Her husband was watching us from a shy distance. She then proposed that if she could find it, she'd give it to me. I didn't want to risk losing out on acquiring another antique, but under the circumstances, I felt compelled not to buy the glass gem in front of her. She said she would go home straightaway and look for it. If luck were to be on our side, she would return and bring it to me at the hotel where I was staying. I gave her my cell number and we departed in different directions from what was now an almost empty flea market. I left with a strange feeling about her.

I went for a short walk and ended up in a park I hadn't yet come across during my many strolls throughout Lisieux. I sauntered along a pebbled path towards a stone archway; there were several such entrances along the periphery of the park. I walked through one of them and turned left. An uneasy feeling took hold of me as I continued down the road. I sensed an approaching force of evil coming from behind the corner fortress wall. I thought about turning back. Many years ago, while I was living in France, I had been followed several times. Memories of those events flooded my mind like rushing waves, carrying thoughts of the peril I surely had escaped.

Just as the ominous feeling of darkness and heaviness in the air grew stronger, my phone rang. Monique, the lady I'd met at the market, was calling me about the antique float. As we spoke, I became further convinced that her purpose, in that moment, was to pull me away from where I was headed.

I quickly returned to my hotel, which was next to a wonderful *patisserie* and teahouse, but there was no time to grab a pastry. I felt like I was waiting to reunite with old friends. As they pulled up to the sidewalk in their grey Peugeot, I could see her through the passenger window. Elated, she quickly got out of their car and handed me a slightly wrinkled, white plastic bag. We spoke briefly. I wanted to ask her for her address in order to send them a thank you note but was hesitant because such information is personal— we were, after all, strangers. We said our goodbyes. There was an awkward pause before she forthrightly asked for my contact information. She continued with an unusual wishfulness in her voice that if ever I were to come back to Lisieux, maybe we could meet again. And with this shared hope, we parted.

I reflected on how we met, her words, and the keepsake she passed on to me. I carefully swaddled, then packed my treasured French souvenir. I was certain that her gesture was more than a mere act of kindness. As I zipped up my suitcase, I had an acute awareness that our encounter would one day serve another purpose. With this strong belief, I left *la belle Normandie*.

I did consider the possibility that one day I might return to their hometown and meet with them again, but never did I imagine that I would call upon them for a favour. I needed to be assured that the monsignor in Lisieux would receive my letter. I didn't want it to get lost in the shuffle or be read by someone other than him. With these concerns, the role of Monique and that of her husband, Roger, would come into play. I had sent them a registered letter wherein I asked if they could kindly hand-deliver my enclosed personal note to the monsignor. I expressed that if it wasn't possible, I'd understand. They agreed to act as my messengers.

I received an email from their son, Eric, the day after the piece of paper had appeared in my front yard. He informed me that his mother had had a rendezvous with the monsignor at 11:30 a.m. on the 26th of November. I was speechless. The day they met was the same day that the piece of paper had surfaced, confirming my belief that my letter had arrived in France. Saint Thérèse was indeed communicating with me that autumn day! I never anticipated, however, that it'd be the exact date that my letter had been placed in the monsignor's hands. My request was heard in Heaven! God has truly blessed me with many special French angels!

*Love consumes us
only in the measure of our self-surrender.*

Saint Thérèse

Within

Many years ago, during one of my darkest times, I felt distressed as I looked at my legs covered with bulging tortuous veins, which always seemed to intrigue the doctors. With stabbing pain and discomfort from my pelvic area down to my ankles, I lay crying in self-pity. I remember exactly where I was: on my bedroom floor, facing a full-length mirror on the wall. Struggling physically, emotionally, and spiritually, it felt like a strenuous climb to rise to my knees. I looked up towards Heaven, and called out to Him in anguish: "God, why have you forsaken me?"

Suddenly and unexpectedly, I stopped crying. Fiercely, I wiped away the remaining tears from my face with a renewed strength and courage that could have come only from Him. I resolved to no longer question, "Why me?" I promised God that with all my imperfections, I would accept what was in store for me and prove my trust in Him.

At this point in my life, I'd had seven surgical interventions, including a dramatic heart surgery where I came close to death for the second time in my life. Tired of experiencing one illness after another and in desperate need of spiritual transformation, I began to search for an understanding of the mysteries of life. I yearned for knowledge of truth and longed to be sustained by a divine force. I began to thirst for a different feeling of connectedness that I had recently discovered in saintly and godly love.

I desire to do your will, my God.

Psalm 40:8a

Here, There, and Everywhere

A few of the many mysteries I've pondered and grown in my understanding over the past five years include: faith, hope, love, trust, trials and tribulations, grace, prayer, darkness, scripture, His promise, miracles, surrender, devotion, holiness, sanctity, martyrdom, suffering, salvation, redemption, transgressions, forgiveness, divinity, humility, separation, consolation, eternal life, purgatory, purification, self-abandonment, the Holy Spirit, Jesus the Saviour, Mary our Mother, human limitations, confidence in the Lord, a merciful loving God, and the communion of angels and saints. From my awakening came my greatest desires—to search for God everywhere in my daily life and to be able to discern His will over my own.

I thought that if my request were to be granted by the monsignor, my next chapter would begin with fascinating stories of grace and healings from around the world attributed to Saint Thérèse.

Tick tock.

I just kept waiting; I didn't perceive how much time had gone by without having heard a word from the monsignor. I imagined it would be fitting that I would receive a response from him one way or the other. To my chagrin, I hadn't heard a word.

Meanwhile, I developed more allergies to medications and continued to suffer physically. As the level of pain increased, I learned to offer up my affliction to the Lord. Patiently, I waited for Him to restore my health. I told God that I was open to learning whatever He must teach me first. My spiritual healing had begun. With a pleading heart, I begged the Divine Healer to mould me and strengthen me in my trials. Remembering Saint Thérèse's ethereal words relieved and encouraged me: "Our Lord isn't anxious for us to suffer so let's not complain to Him any more than is necessary! He sees us in our misery and looks forward to our final victory. If we could only appreciate the great work He's doing in preparing these crosses for us."[30]

Tick tock.

I continue to wait on the Lord with great expectancy.

---

[30]   Fr. Loren Gonzales. "Seven Disguises In Which God Frequently Sends His Graces." Overheard in the Sacristy. Thursday, February 1, 2007. Retrieved from fiftysophomoricsummers.blog-spot.com/search?q=our+lord+is+not+anxious.

... that I may always long for you alone,
who are the bread of angels
and the fulfillment of the soul's deepest desires ...

Saint Bonaventure

Happy Birthday

My birthday came wrapped in splendour, ablaze with vibrant colours and intense emotion. I sensed the presence of Saint Thérèse that autumn day. She was smiling down on me from Heaven, the place to which I often looked in need, awe, and gratitude. Perceiving her spirit was another privileged moment, like all the others.

By sheer happenstance, I received an email that marvellous day from Maureen O'Riordan, a long-time student of Saint Thérèse and curator of the outstanding website Saint Therese of Lisieux: A Gateway. I learned of her while browsing the internet seeking information about Saint Thérèse. From time to time, I had the pleasure of exchanging emails with Maureen. She asked me if I'd be interested in translating a French document from the archives of the Carmel of Lisieux for publication on her website. Words were insufficient to express my surprise and happiness to read her request. This valued document had been carefully preserved in France for one hundred years. A copy of it was now readily accessible to me. Overcome with emotion, I went before the tabernacle to pray in thankfulness before reading the documented testimonies.

Perhaps Saint Thérèse wanted me to have special first-hand knowledge of these triumphant events. I believed that I had been given the article "Eyewitness Accounts of the Exhumation of the Relics of Saint Therese of Lisieux"[31] to translate because it was impossible for me to gain access to the letters of miracles sent to the Carmel. After all, she provided me with a sign—through the appearance of the piece of paper the day when my letter was received by the French monsignor—to let me know that she was aware of my aspirations. Details of the events that I was curious about when I was at her gravesite were given to me to translate into English for the first time in history. I soon learned how this unexpected and extraordinary birthday gift would also serve as another part of His plan.

[31]   O'Riordan, Maureen, ed. "Eyewitness Accounts of the Exhumations of the Relics of St. Therese of Lisieux" from the Archives of the Carmel of Lisieux. Trans. Monique Pilon-Fraschetti for Saint Therese of Lisieux: A Gateway, www.thereseoflisieux.org, October 19, 2010. http://www.thereseoflisieux.org/st-therese-relics-return-to-ca/.

Nothing is far from God.

Saint Monica

Trust

Slightly rusted, cast-iron urns that stand on either side of my family home's front door overflowed with fresh pine and large pinecones. Fresh wreaths with velvet bows decorated each of our six windows. Several hanging baskets cascaded with fir and spruce clippings, emitting the fragrance of a wintry Christmas. Shiny silver-coloured ornaments filled the emptied water fountain and dangled from the three arbours that embellish our pathway to the backyard. I asked myself how almost a year could've already gone by since I had decorated the house for the holidays—the time when my request was hand-delivered to a French monsignor.

I wanted to feel more in sync with *God's time.* Faithfully, I continued to wait on Him. Physically, I suffered horribly throughout this period. At times, feeling dispirited, the days passed slowly. I endured extreme moments of pain when I thought

I could bear no more. If it were not for my belief in *my miracle*, I'm not sure what would have become of me. The light of hope did flicker, but it never lost its flame. God sustained me, and I knew His saints were with me—praying for me.

During this time, my spiritual adviser, Fr. Beaune, had given me a book entitled *Miracles Do Happen* by Sister Briege McKenna. Drawn by her personal story, remarkable worldwide ministry, and contemplations on the living Christ, I became further interested in the mystery of the Real Presence of the Eucharist. The idea of spending time in front of the Blessed Sacrament and tabernacle was relatively new to me. Early-century saints had placed tremendous emphasis on Eucharistic Adoration. They claimed that frequent visits before the Sacrament of the Altar greatly help souls, giving them peace and strength. Saint Alphonsus of Liguori said, "But you will find that all the Saints were enamoured of this most sweet devotion; … . Only try this devotion, and by experience you will see the great benefits that you will derive from it."[32] I decided to visit Jesus more often in hope of experiencing these blessings.

Sister Briege travelled the world at a rapid pace. After I first learned of her, it would be ten months before she'd return to North America. I felt excited about the prospect of attending her one-day retreat in early December—a date that was fast approaching. Before having read about her prayer and healing event in Clearwater, Florida, I had written to an archivist in Lisieux, whom I shall call Sister Eloïse. I informed her that I was the translator of the document detailing the eyewitness accounts

---

[32] Alphonsus Liguori, *Visits to the Most Holy Sacrament and The Blessed Virgin Mary*, ed. R.A. Coffin, (London: Burns & Lamber, 1855). 8, 9.

of Saint Thérèse's exhumations. I spoke of my devotion to our dear saint and my desire to obtain access to the inspirational letters sent to the Carmel. One evening, a strong urge came over me to pray these words to Mary and Saint Thérèse: *I want to see Sister Briege but I only want to go if God wants me there. I would like a sign. If He wants me to meet her, I would like a response from the Carmel of Lisieux tomorrow, Saturday!* With intensity, I repeated this exact supplication twice.

Flight prices were increasing, and fewer retreat registrations were being accepted as seats were almost sold out. I was tempted to book my flight, but, with confidence, I refrained from buying my airline ticket. I decided to wait and see if I would receive my sign.

Morning dawned crisp and bright. The clarity of the vivid blue sky, the rising sun, and the refreshing cool air entering through our opened windows awoke in me a spirit of enthusiasm for the day that lay ahead. My children were playing happily and quietly. I made myself a coffee, then turned on my computer without anticipating receiving any message in particular—my prayer request from the day before hadn't entered my mind so early in the morning.

A notification popped up on my screen indicating that I had one letter in my inbox. I clicked the stamp icon. The words "Carmel of Lisieux," written in bold print, leapt off the page. I closed my eyes and then reopened them just to make sure that what I saw was real and still there.

It was ... and my heart may have even skipped a beat.

The Lord is near.

Philippians 4:5b

Divine Timing

The weeks following receipt of Sister Eloïse's email were filled with torrents of physical pain and far too many days spent in bed. I felt comforted recalling the morning when I had opened her email. Before reading the response that day, I had glanced at the bottom of the note to see who had written to me. Eagerly, I had called out to my children, "The archivist wrote! The archivist wrote!" Without delay, I heard the quick shuffling sound of their footsteps pattering softly towards me as I cheered, "I have an answer from the Carmel! Sister Eloïse wrote to me!" I welcomed my daughter's warm embrace, which was accompanied by her sweet whispered sigh, "Oh mom!" I then tried to read the email, but my tears interfered. I dried my eyes and paused for a moment to reflect on how I might feel if this long-awaited answer was *no*.

Sister Eloïse couldn't grant me publishing rights or access to the letters. She justified her response by explaining that the intent of those who submit letters to the Carmel is to share their personal story of grace and not necessarily to have them published. Her reason made perfect sense and was one I had considered as a potential obstacle to my request. Recognizing my interest in miracles, she provided me with the names of books and websites where I could read similar stories. She ended her message with well-wishes, appreciation for my translation, and prayers for my intentions.

A year had passed without receiving a reply from the monsignor. Clearly, I was meant to translate the article and then be in touch with a more suitable contact—a religious archivist. The sequence of events all happened for a reason. I then prepared myself for the retreat and the mystery that lay ahead.

I was going to a place where God wanted me to be.

*Whoever believes in me
will do the works I have been doing,
and they will do even greater things than these.*

John 14:12a

Clearwater, Florida, 2011

Happily, I stowed away my UGGS in exchange for jewelled flip-flops, down jackets were traded for summer clothing, and winter hats swapped for motif baseball caps.

I landed in Fort Myers, Florida, feeling serene. Immediately upon exiting the airport terminal, I welcomed the sunshine and balmy weather. The palm leaves rustled carelessly, a slight sound perceptible only to the unaccustomed visitor. The breeze tickled through my hair. I could smell the tropical ocean air from the airport. Cheerfully, my *zio* Dante greeted me. He looked radiant. I have always referred to him as my *uncle*, even though we aren't truly related. He has loved me dearly since I was a little girl, from as far back as I can remember.

A week before I arrived, he had hurt his back and was unable to move. He hadn't previously disclosed his unfortunate condition as he didn't want me to be concerned about our ability to attend the retreat, which was 212 kilometres away. He went as far as asking a few friends if they would be willing to take us to the event should he be unable to drive. He had received a spinal injection two days before my arrival. The specialist had told him that it would be days before the medicine would take effect, if it worked at all. Determined to attend the retreat, he stayed awake all night, meditating on an image of the Madonna. With devotion, he prayed for her intercession.

The next morning, he discovered he could move. He spoke with great enthusiasm about how the treatment was given with such accuracy, how the results were quicker than expected, and how Mary had surely listened to his fervent prayers the night before. He had been bedridden for days but was now completely pain-free. He danced a few steps, shuffling to a tune that seemed to come from within. His luminous face portrayed his inner peace. His energy was vibrant and contagious. Never in my whole life had I seen him quite like this. He already seemed transformed.

The morning after my late afternoon arrival, we departed for the retreat. I was halfway out the door when I stepped back to the large crystal bowl filled with Dove chocolates waiting to be snatched. They were individually wrapped in shiny foil, in the colours of burnt orange and Persian rose. While en route, I unwrapped my first one. The message written on the inside of the foil read: "Be strong. The cure is near." Dante's immediate reaction was of keen excitement, interlaced with joyous laughter. Once he quieted, we furtively stole a glance at one another. The twinkle in his eyes and the emotion in his heart could not be concealed.

No words were exchanged, just distinct giggles full of hope and wonder. It was clear: we were both secretly hoping the message would prove prophetic. During the drive, he shared stories that I had never heard before. Often, he interrupted himself with bubbly chatter about how great he felt; even the fact that he had cancer seemed to vanish.

Though Dante accompanied me in friendship, this trip's purpose was not meant for me alone. I felt it again: miracle or not, it didn't matter. We were together and our shared moments were more than enough.

Sister Briege's charisma was splashed with a dash of humanity. While radiating hope, peace, and an unfaltering trust in the Lord, she shared wonderful stories with humour and humility. She spoke effortlessly and fascinatingly. God's hand was at work in her life. The day was uplifting and inspirational. We met another one of God's servants, Father Kevin Scallon, who led the healing service and preached the gospel. Criss-crossing every continent together, they have ministered around the world for over thirty years. Together, they have witnessed the slums of Brazil and underground China, proclaimed in oppressive places, visited impoverished small towns, and provided retreats for the laity and priests in the Eternal City and beyond. With Delta Air Lines alone, they have flown over a million miles; I wish I could have tagged along. Their international, fast-paced schedule indicates an incredible energy.

Clearwater is beautifully situated on the west coast. The shimmering ocean added a sense of tranquility to the calm that already prevailed. After morning mass, we walked the grounds bestrewn with palms and intertwined with a species of weeping trees I had never seen before. A few fountains, a small white bridge over a pond, and statues representing the Stations of the Cross made an idyllic setting for a spiritual retreat. The breeze carried a hint of saltiness and it mixed with the smell that emanated from the old tree under which we sat and ate our lunch. Sitting in partial shade, I welcomed the warmth of the filtering sunbeams as they danced upon us through the moving leaves.

During this pause in the day, Sister Briege had agreed to a book signing. People were purchasing books and had formed a queue. Upon hearing a stranger announce, "Here is your best customer," I looked up as I was trying to juggle my wallet, dangling purse, and six books I had bought. At first, I didn't realize that he was referring to me nor that these words were directed to the author herself. Before my eyes was Sister Briege. She stood there, looking at me. I was taken by complete surprise. I think I said, "Hello." I first noted her glow and then her assertive blue-grey eyes—full of conviction. Books in hand, I hoped she noticed that I was a fan.

After our brief encounter, she sat at a table, ready to begin the signing session. As I waited my turn, I watched her interact with her followers. She patiently acknowledged each person with genuine interest. Praying differently over each one, both in gesture and in word, she either placed her hand above their heads, on their foreheads, or held their hand in hers. To a select few, she gifted small turquoise Miraculous Medals, which she kept tucked away in the pocket of her brown habit.

I asked a woman standing behind me in line if she wouldn't mind taking a few photos of me and Sister Briege when it was my turn to have my books signed. The woman and I spoke briefly. I detected a past struggle and a present abandon, blended with the perfect dose of hope. Noticing that she didn't have a camera, I offered to take some pictures of her with the author and promised to send them to her.

Inconspicuously, she snapped pictures rapidly—like a *paparazzo*. As Sister Briege and I conversed, she paused for a moment to admire my baroque-styled rosary necklace. She wasn't the first to notice it for its meaning, beauty, and unique design. Respectfully, she lifted the bejewelled medal and cross and inspected them in her palm. With confidence, she claimed, "You are wearing the greatest protection you could ever wear." She was referring to the Miraculous Medal, like the one she gave to those in line. In 1830, Saint Catherine Labouré had a vision of the Blessed Virgin, who instructed her to have a medal designed with the specifications that she provided. Special graces are said to be given to those who wear it with faith and devotion, especially at the hour of their death. I closed my eyes and silently presented my heartfelt prayers for the healing of friends, family, and self. With a gentle, compassionate hand, she made the sign of the cross on my forehead. A moment later, she performed this same gesture above my heart. Words and smiles were intermittently exchanged as she signed the books. She reached deep into her side pocket and then placed four Miraculous Medals of my favourite colour into my hand.

Several weeks after the retreat, Dante was still exuberant! Whenever I spoke to him, my spirits were lifted for at least a day. His energy was transmitted over the phone from a thousand miles away. I had never seen or heard someone feel so renewed and enlivened. Hearing and listening to his voice, intoxicated with optimism, brought me joy. With laughter, he affirmed, "I'm fine. I'm fine. I have Jesus with me now!"

Yes, he has Jesus with him now.

If I could reach up and hold a Star
for every time you've made me smile,
the entire evening sky would be
in the palm of my hand.

Author Unknown

Transcendental Moments

The nine months that followed the healing event in Clearwater felt like a hundred years due to my chronic debilitating pain. This period, however, was filled with mysterious occurrences during which I experienced God's divinity—manifestations of His love, glory, and presence. He blessed me with an incomparable sign—sparkles. The notion of receiving them was incomprehensible. Nonetheless, I knew of its authenticity because it happened to me.

I documented most of these supernatural instances of receiving sparkles which, at last count, had occurred over an astounding 114 consecutive days. Although, I will never be able to give justice to these ineffable moments of grace, this truth remains: I wish I had kept a complete, detailed diary archiving how I felt, along with the dates, times, and places where these phenomena happened. I regret not jotting down such descriptions in a Florentine-embossed, leather-bound book, for my sake or posterity's, even if left unread.

From time to time, I attended a prayer group at the home of a lovely couple. Some fifty devotees gather to praise, sing, and share stories of God's infinite love, mercy, and power. One evening, I noticed that I had fine glitter on the palms of my hands. I thought to myself, *that's strange! What did I touch? Where was it from? Did it come from the exterior of my glass of water?* I had touched nothing else. This novel, beautiful, shimmering glitter appeared solely on the palms of my hands. I didn't think of asking anyone about what I saw. In truth, afterwards, I'd even forgotten about it, and only later—after learning of its origin—did I recall that it had happened on three previous occasions while I was at prayer group.

Someone had announced at our get-together that the Holy Spirit had come and that we should look at the palms of our hands. I thought, *what an assured and grateful declaration!* I looked at my palms, which were covered in tiny, ultra-fine, brilliant, sparkles— unmistakably like the ones I'd received before! *They came from God Himself?* I was mystified and overwhelmed. They were given to only a few of us that night. Baffled, I drove home, barely touching the steering wheel, hopeful the glitter would remain for a while. I was speechless, yet I wanted to scream this revelation to the whole world, even if whoever heard me might conclude that I had lost my mind. In the end, I shared these intimate experiences only with a few discreet people.

The sparkles appeared exclusively on the palms of my hands; there was no evidence of any on my clothing or anywhere around me. To eliminate my initial doubt of the glitter's origin, I made sure not to wear makeup, washed my hands before going to prayer group, and once there, avoided coming into contact with anything. Often, when we gathered to worship, I received a dusting of glitter. The Lord bestowed me with hundreds of them—perhaps thousands—when I would meet and pray with my spiritual adviser, attend mass, during my increased visits to the tabernacle, and, several times, in the privacy of my own home. Oh, what sweet divine consolation! Their beauty is unsurpassable. They convey an indefinable love—a transcendent love. My soul was convinced of their source, overshadowing the light of all human reason.

Whenever Father Beaune and I would meet, we always recited the Divine Mercy Chaplet. Every time after we prayed, I received sparkles. My palms and fingertips would become completely covered in them. Their brilliance was extraordinary. One time, the interiors of my hands were entirely bejewelled in silvery-pink, opalescent splendour. Overjoyed, I raced home, pulled hastily into the driveway, leapt out of my car, and dashed towards my husband, who was standing directly in the sunlight and visibly alarmed by my actions. Without a word, I extended my palms up towards his eyes. My children and their friend rushed over from across the street, incited by the commotion. When I asked the neighbourhood boy what he saw, he candidly confirmed, "Sparkles! There are so many! Where did you get them?" My daughter and son remained silent. Their delighted smiles and beaming eyes secretly expressed a multitude of words. Over time, they also had their own experience receiving sparkles when we attended mass.

It had been suggested by a friend that I try to preserve the glitter on a piece of clear tape. I liked the idea—maybe there'd come a time when I would share them with someone in need. On a day that the sparkles appeared particularly resplendent, I asked my daughter to try and conserve them. Intently inspecting my hands, she meticulously and superbly collected the sparkles. I didn't anticipate that it would be the first and last time they could be removed from my skin. From that moment on, they only appeared underneath my skin. Father Beaune, in his wisdom, explained that this could only mean one thing: they were intended solely for me. Radiant, shimmering sparkles from God were given according to His will.

On the twenty-seventh consecutive day of receiving glitter, I examined them for a long time. I was completely consumed by their beauty. The amount of love and peace that flowed from them into my heart was staggering. I couldn't bear this abundance of love; it was too overwhelming for my soul. A saint once asserted that God reveals His love a little at a time because if He showed it all at once, one could not bear it. Yet receiving this amount of love was more than my heart could hold.

Each time He lavished me with this visible sign of His presence, I felt loved and at peace. For months, I trekked daily to church through winter snowstorms and freezing temperatures. I longed for the sparkles. I admit even becoming greedy, hoping and asking for them. Over time, visiting the tabernacle out of my own needs, began to decrease. Instead, I went and meditated before Him, asking *how I could better serve Him. What was my Saviour's path for me? The one I did not understand or foresee?* I begged Him for answers.

Whenever I visited Him at the tabernacle or attended mass, I received a sprinkling of glitter. Each time, its magnificence overtook and diminished me. Regretfully, I didn't track all the times this phenomenon occurred. Inadequately, I search for words to describe how I felt receiving His grace. On one occasion, I was in deep, unreserved prayer and not thinking the least bit about receiving sparkles. I opened my eyes and happened to glance down at my clasped hands. For the first-time, the backsides were covered in sparkles. They looked like they had been dipped in silvery-white glitter. I will never forget that for which I prayed. He saw my brokenness, heard my inexhaustible cries, and wiped away my tears through this glorious anointing. The power of His love moved me beyond words.

Another time, when I was in front of the Tabernacle, one white sparkle appeared in the centre of my palm and shone with an indescribable brilliance. I had never seen or experienced anything like it. I was pulled into its infinite radiance. The universe and all of eternity was at its centre. Its vastness and limitlessness went through me as I was being drawn towards it. The sacredness of this light became me, and I became it. Its luminosity and existence were beyond comprehension. I didn't want to leave the church that day because, on past occasions, the moment I'd exit the doors, the sparkles would disappear from my hands. I could have remained there forever, in its permeating, immaculate light.

Peace I leave with you; my peace I give you.
I do not give to you as the world gives.

John 14:27

Saint Paul, Minnesota, 2011

Kelsey, my niece and godchild, enjoyed listening to the stories of how I lifted my prayers to Saint Thérèse and how my novenas were answered. Intrigued by how she fulfills her promise of making God loved and letting "fall a shower of roses,"[33] Kelsey decided to choose *Thérèse* for her Confirmation name. I had the pleasure of being her sponsor and attending the ceremony at the Cathedral of Saint Paul in the Twin Cities.

She was anointed with her first dusting of sparkles during the liturgy. She was awed by the power of the Holy Spirit and the majesty of receiving sparkles. Astonished, she affectionately hugged me several times throughout the mass. Tears flooded her

---

[33]   Thérèse, *The Story of a Soul*, 213.

ocean-blue eyes. What glory—the Holy Spirit not only descended upon her as part of receiving the Sacrament of Confirmation but also manifested a visible sign.

We celebrated the occasion at an Italian restaurant. As we followed the hostess, I immediately noticed faux flowers in baskets on the low-lying enclosure alongside our table. Nowhere else in the restaurant was it decorated this way. I didn't think much of it other than that it looked like a balcony with nice flowers. I had not made any symbolic connection, until, from a closer proximity, I spotted a framed picture hanging on the Roman pillar next to our table. I quickly motioned to my niece to come towards me. Attentively, she rushed to my side. "Look!" I whispered, while casting a glance towards the small photo. Her eyes widened with surprise upon seeing the classical depiction of Saint Thérèse of the Child Jesus holding a crucifix and roses. How wondrous that these signs of her presence were provided so quickly. I thought back to when I saw the reproduction photo of Santa Teresa at the restaurant in Madrid and assured Kelsey that signs such as these were of no coincidence, and more would follow.

During the mass, her sister Alyssa also received sparkles. The iridescent glitter appeared beneath her skin. The following morning, well after her evening shower, she discovered they were still visible, shimmering. Together, we stared at her palms. The sanctification she received was remarkable. I couldn't have foreseen that the sparkles would remain with her throughout the night. She went to school that day and showed her hands to her friends. They immediately looked at their palms in hopes of seeing the same.

Even now I know it:
yes, all my hopes will be fulfilled …
yes … the Lord will work wonders for me
which will surpass infinitely
my immeasurable desires.

Saint Thérèse's VIII Letter to Mère Agnès de Jésus

Here and Now

I adore many saints.

I am incapable of fully expressing the sentiments that dwell in my heart for Saint Thérèse, my eternal sister and friend who hears my every whisper. The Lord blessed the world with her soul and immeasurable love. Knowing all too well of my spiritual needs, He sent her forth into my life.

I love Saint Bernadette Soubirous for her courage and faithfulness, for having answered my mother's plea that she stand before Mary with a prayer to spare my life at birth, and for having called me to Lourdes where I would receive an unparalleled and supernatural sign at the Massabielle Grotto.

I cherish the humble and beloved Saint Anthony for having saved the souls of Padova, for the wondrous miracles he performed, for his exquisite qualities, for his abundance of love for God and humanity, and for always hearing my requests and those of others.

I admire Saint Francis of Assisi for how he traded in a life of riches for one of poverty; for his love of nature and animals; and for instantly answering our impassioned intercessory prayer for our injured cat, Marshmellow, by visibly curing his condition on the word "Amen!"

I treasure and adore two of the seven archangels who stand before the throne of God: Archangel Michael, whose powerful aid supremely and magnificently protects me; and Archangel Raphael, noble and mighty messenger from on High, whose refuge, guidance, and intercession in my life have been–and continue to be—exceptional. I have felt his wings envelop me. These archangels have undoubtedly responded to my prayers in sovereign ways. What assurance I have in calling upon them! With, and through them, I magnify the Lord.

Over the years, I have also implored Saints Luke, Jude, Paul, Claire, Lucia, Joseph, Gerard, Monica, Stanislas, Apollonia, Peregrine, John Vianney, Vincent de Paul, Frances de Sales, John of the Cross, Catherine of Siena, Augustine of Hippo, Thomas of Aquinas, Mary Magdalene, Catherine Labouré, Théophane Venard, Teresa of Avila, Blessed Father Solaneus Casey, and Blessed Zélie Martin and Blessed Louis Martin, who have since become saints. Their lives inspire me. They listen, console, protect, intercede, and reconcile. I extol communing with them in hope, trust, gratitude, and love. I am completely empty without them.

I want to further feel the hand of God upon me. I hope to feel His warmth travel through me, as known to be experienced by those who receive instantaneous, miraculous healings. Should He so choose, He will cure me. If my desire, however, is not in accordance with His will, I know He will still provide me with other graces.

Are you aware that you are under His divine gaze in all circumstances? Do you believe He is always there? Watching over you in your darkest nights? I assure you, *he's not asleep in the boat.*[34] Do you want to discover these truths? Pray without ceasing. Seek Him relentlessly until you find Him. He is there waiting. Turn to Him in enduring faith, absolute trust, and complete self-abandon. He offers a spiritual life to every soul, through His promise, "… I am the way, the truth and the life."[35] Know that to follow Him is the ultimate path for He is the only one true compass, the Lord of Lords, who calls us each by name!

---

[34]   Matthew 8:24 (World English Bible).

[35]   John 14:6 (WEB).

*For he will command his angels concerning you
to guard you in all your ways.*

Psalm 91:11

Light in the Darkness

My angel story referenced in the Preface has been shared with family and close friends. Amazed and captivated by my description of how the night unfolded when I met an angel, they have often asked me to repeat the supernatural event to them or share it with their friends. I have, thus, decided to recount in more detail what transpired that late shivery December night when even the pale, grey moon seemed to hide behind sparse clouds.

In case you didn't read the section about my encounter with an angel, I will present the portrait of her again: she was an aged, curved beggar, cloaked in tattered, grey, wool clothing with a matching frayed knitted tuque nestled just above her squinted blue eyes. She looked at me pleadingly. Her empty, humble hands were wrapped in shredded knit hobo gloves. I wish I had understood at the time who she was and held her hands in mine with warm recognition. On a desolate pathway, she mysteriously appeared out of nowhere, then disappeared, after saving me from a menacing Frenchman!

During the spring of 1985, I spent my two-week Easter break discovering Paris for the first time. On occasion, a friend and I zigzagged around the City of Lights on his motorcycle. Enamoured with the sites, I was thrilled to be going along the Avenue Champs-Elysée and every other street in between. New Year's Eve was different, I found myself alone. I could have remained in the small town where I had enjoyed Christmas festivities with distant relatives, but I decided to return to the big city where I was studying. Ringing in the New Year carries the expectation of holiday cheer and, living in France, it was easy to fantasize about what it would be like to indulge in a sports holiday in the French Alps—spending the evening with old friends in a cozy chalet or toasting with new ones in an après-ski nightclub after skiing the slopes of Chamonix. Oh, the reverie of promenading in Nice or Saint Tropez, with the allure of dressing in silk or sequins and being draped in a luxurious, winter-white cashmere cape, with a touch of glitter added around smoky eyes—all to reflect being on the glitzy, glamorous seaside in southeastern France!

The Alpine Mountains and the French Riviera propose idealistic opportunities to say goodbye to the old and to welcome the new, but thoughts of celebrating in these places quickly went adrift as if swept away by a cascading avalanche or crushed by the waves of the crystal-clear Mediterranean Sea itself. The reality was, I was a foreign student running low on funds and these ideas were just dreams of a much younger and different me. Most of my classmates had returned to their respective homes for the holidays—Amsterdam, small towns in Germany and Korea, Chile, too. I didn't know whether or not the group who always smiled and nodded as they greeted me with an enthusiastic "Konnichiwa" had returned to their motherland, Japan. Looking back, I should have become acquainted with them beyond our informal "hello" at midday.

After descending steep and winding roads, I arrived at the city centre an hour or so before the clock struck twelve. I wanted to see the elaborately adorned fir tree in the royal Place Stanislas square. I was living in Nancy, Lorraine, 130 kilometres northwest from Sélestat, Alsace, where the first outdoor decorated Christmas tree appeared in France in 1521. During this period, pines were decorated with red apples to symbolize the temptation of Adam and Eve and wafers resembling Eucharistic Hosts to represent redemption.[36] Even to this day, the almost 500-year-old tradition of displaying a tree in the town square is not taken for granted. The Nancéiens were talking about it as if it were a novelty. I didn't, however, even make my way close to the enormous tree to see it in all its grandeur.

As far as I can remember, there was a stand adjacent to the golden arch that leads to the Parc de la Pépinière. I would often pick up a freshly made waffle there, on my way to the park. In France, they are served more as a snack than for breakfast, so they would surely be for sale at this late hour. I did not, however, make it to buy one. Not long after I had entered the square, I began to feel uneasy. The twinkling Christmas lights seemed to dim, and

---

[36]   Pierre Guernier. "The Top Traditions of the French Christmas Tree." "What are the Christmas tree decorations in France?" French moments, February 7, 2022. https://frenchmoments.eu/french-christmas-tree-le-sapin-de-noel-en-france/.

the merriment of the people walking around began to fade into the bleakness of the night.

Place Stanislas was built to connect the medieval *old town* of Nancy with the seventeenth century *new town* that were once separated by marshland. I don't recall from which gilded wrought-iron corner gate I had entered, nor through which end of the square I had later escaped.

Looking at a boutique window display, I noticed the reflection of a white Peugeot deliberately passing by. My senses were awakened, which seemed to not only magnify the size of the car but also slow down time. I turned around for a clearer view, at which point, I caught more than the back end of the suspicious vehicle. My eyes locked with the driver's in his rear-view mirror; instantly his spoke menacingly, and, while mine remained focused, I wasn't sure what they revealed to him. Immediately, I stepped back and tried to blend in with the people around me. A moment later, I looked around to see if this sinister man was still in sight. He was; I spotted his car in the distance. He appeared to be circling back around towards me. I pretended to continue to window-shop as I tried to figure out my getaway plan. In retrospect, I should have come up with a much better one.

Out of the corner of my eye and with my back to the road, I saw him in his car, approaching towards my right. Boldly, I turned to face him straight on. This was not part of my exit strategy. As he slowly drove by, I could see him through the passenger window, hunched over, tightly gripping the steering wheel, his body pressed up against it with his shoulders slightly angled towards his right side. He peered at me with beady, disturbing eyes. It was time for me to leave.

Swiftly, I started to walk in the opposite direction to which he was driving. I naively thought this would buy me some time. The square is framed by five magnificent buildings with palatial balconies and ornate fountains in two of the corners. I wasn't near the Neptune Fountain, the Grand Hôtel de la Reine, or the Nancy and Lorraine Opera House that faced one of the oldest museums in France—the Musée des Beaux-Arts de Nancy. I wasn't near City Hall, and I don't recall walking through the Arc de Triomphe nearby, which links Place Stanislas to Place de la Carrière, but I distinctly remember the linden trees because it was from in-between the trunks that I saw him park his car.

I wasn't near the Palais du Gouvernement because the façade wasn't illuminated and surely a government palace would have been well lit up at night. I gather that I must have entered Place d'Alliance, the smallest of the three connected squares. It was the first time I had ever been in this area. Even though it was only two hundred metres from Place Stanislas, it felt far removed. I don't remember the route I took to arrive. I cannot retrace in my mind having walked that distance, but I do know that with each step my surroundings became quieter and darker.

I no longer heard any chatter or traffic. I was completely alone until I saw the Peugeot pull up no more than sixty metres to my right. I continued onwards through the rectangular path surrounded by linden trees. If I turned back, it would become obvious that I had no clear destination. His car door slammed shut.

Crunch. Crunch. Crunch.

He was walking towards me, stepping heavily on the pebbles. The sound grew faster and louder. Before I knew it, he was behind me, advancing closer. I could hear him breathe. I walked assertively, acting as though I knew where I was headed. But I was in an unfamiliar place and had no clue where to go. In French, he said, "Oh, but you are walking faster now!"

Somehow, I confidently answered, "You can leave me alone now!"

With a thrilled tone, he affirmed, *"Ah, mais vous-êtes étrangière!"* ("Ah, but you are a foreigner!") My accent gave me away. Now he was walking right beside me, in unison with my step, glaring at me.

Through the leafless trees with their tightly woven branches, I could see several windows of the three-floored building that spanned the length of the left side of the square. Strangely, everyone who lived there must have either been asleep or not home because all the lights were off, and the drapes were drawn. The apartments on the right side were too far for me to run towards in hope that someone could provide protection. Straight ahead of us was another building that also seemed lifeless. There was a road to the left side, but it looked like it led into the abyss. I had nowhere to turn, and that's when I said, "God, please, help me!"

Suddenly, out of nowhere, an aged, curved beggar appeared in front of us. Immediately, I wondered from where she could have come. I had just finished surveying the area, looking for a place of refuge or a person to whom I could call out for help. There had been no one around and I would have noticed her silhouette approaching; instead, she arose a mere metre and a half away from us. She wore a charcoal-grey wool sweater that looked as if it had endured many seasons. With a wooden cane in her right hand, she took a few steps forward. Stunned, we stood motionless as we watched her. With an open-faced palm, she outstretched her hand in the hope of receiving alms. She raised it further towards me, paused at the level of my heart, then lifted it higher as she curled her fingers inward, forming a cup. She asked, *"Avez-vous des sous? Des sous pour du pain?"* I couldn't believe my ears. I shook my head and replied, *"Non,"* all the while saying to God, "This is who you send me?"

I imagined us from an aerial view. We formed the shape of a triangle. I was looking at her; she was looking back at me, and the ominous man was staring at her, listening attentively with furrowed brows. He wore a peculiar expression. We were both confounded by her but for different reasons. The entire situation caught me off guard. I didn't consider being charitable. I didn't reach into my pocket in search of change so that she could buy bread. At that moment, I was in danger and didn't think that her needs were as urgent as mine.

The air felt crisp. When we spoke to each other, our breath turned into little white misty puffs of air. Like clouds, they floated between us and then dissipated into the darkness. Abruptly, but quietly, the man turned sideways and began to walk away. Just like that. His fierce eyes had turned nonthreatening. They were filled with fear and astonishment. Speechless, he looked like he had seen a ghost.

I watched him as he left, to see where he was headed. His posture and pace reassured me that he was not going to come back. I turned to the old woman, but she was gone. My eyes scanned the vicinity. She was nowhere to be seen. For her to have walked away that quickly in any direction would have been impossible. She had vanished, faster than when she had appeared. I peeked over my right shoulder, relieved to see the French man driving away.

I left Place d'Alliance and never returned. I made my way back to Place Stanislas without any recollection of how I got there. I found myself at a bus stop, hoping to catch the last bus. I searched my pockets and found the exact amount of change required. Once seated, I slunk down to hide. Only then did I begin to tremble. Thankfully, my stop was directly across from where I lived. Exiting the bus, I looked to my right and left for his Peugeot; in doing so, I slipped down the steps on my bottom and fell right out of the bus, landing on my knees. I wondered what the bus driver must have thought—*too much bubbly?* I could hear the exhaling and hissing sound of the doors closing. I dashed towards my apartment building, fumbled with my keys, opened the exterior glass door, and bolted towards the stairs.

Thirty-five years have passed since that cold wintry night in France. It took me more than half that time to realize what had truly transpired that obscure evening. I had often wondered why the predator stood there the way he did, why he stared at the poor woman the way he did, and why he looked at her in a straight direction rather than downwards—she was, after all, quite a bit shorter than him. Through spiritual growth and stories shared, I came to understand that the baffling encounter with the enigmatic woman, and God's response to my plea for help, was a most extraordinary event.

I told my friends Nina and Lori about the Frenchman and the mysterious beggar who saved me from peril. Nina then shared a story about a murderer, a dead woman, and a witness who helped identify the killer. The witness realized, according to the timing of events, that she had been at the scene of the abduction just moments before it had occurred. She wondered why the criminal hadn't chosen her. The police interrogated the perpetrator on her behalf. They asked him why he hadn't taken the woman, who was alone and had passed him before his victim had crossed his path. He answered, "Why would I have? She had two large men walking on either side of her!"

We stopped sipping our cappuccinos and looked at each other. Nina then proposed the idea that maybe I perceived the woman as frail and in need so that I wouldn't become frightened, and that the dangerous Frenchman didn't see her as she had appeared to me. She continued, suggesting that perhaps he saw a strong man, maybe even a police officer. She concluded that we must have also heard different words. This seemed reasonable because a fragile, destitute woman could not have posed a threat to him; asking for change would not have imposed fear causing him to turn away and leave. I was stumped for years but finally understood why the man and I reacted differently when we met her. My friends and I smiled at one another and nodded in mutual understanding as we dug our forks into our desserts, each taking a moment to reflect.

God's light prevailed over the darkness that New Year's Eve I spent in France. I will always marvel at how an angel, disguised as one of us, was sent from Heaven to shield me from danger. My simple call, "God, please help me!" turned out to be a prayer that He answered in a way I couldn't have ever imagined!

Epilogue

Growing up, my mother would recount the story about the time my paediatrician carried me out to the waiting room, lifted me high in the air and, smiling broadly, announced to his patients, "Here's my miracle baby!" The room grew silent. After he was sure that he had captured everyone's attention, he brought me back to the examination room with joy. My mother, surprised by his unexpected actions, followed him proudly.

I was an Rh-positive factor baby. Having Rh-hemolytic disease meant that my blood and my mother's were incompatible. As a result, my mother made Rh antibodies that were attacking and destroying my red blood cells. I was at risk for heart failure, paralysis, brain damage, and even death.

I needed an intrauterine intravascular transfusion to replace my red blood cells. In Canada, the first successful transfusions of this kind were performed in a few large cities between 1964 and late 1966. Real-time ultrasound fetal guidance technology wasn't pioneered until the 1970s.[37] I was born in 1966, not from a big city, and didn't have a multidisciplinary team of highly trained specialists. Since there were serious inherent risks with the procedure and I could have been punctured anywhere on my body with grave consequences, my mother felt that the doctor performing the injection must have been guided from Heaven. My condition also required an exchange transfusion after my birth, and I spent over a month in an incubator.

Against many odds, I survived.

While in hospital, my mother watched the movie *The Song of Bernadette*, which depicts the life of a peasant French girl, Bernadette Soubirous, who has visions of the Virgin Mary; more precisely, "The Immaculate Conception."[38] Moved by the story, my mother prayed to Saint Bernadette, imploring her to intercede so that I would live. Since my parents were both convinced that my mother's prayers were heard, they gave me the middle name Bernadette in recognition of the part she played in my survival and healing.

I have faced medical issues since before I was born, and I've had numerous health concerns throughout my life, but God has always been there for me.

While I was nursing our second child, our then one-month-old son, I sensed that the right side of my face had begun to droop. I felt it sag and then couldn't open my right eye. I tried to call out to

---

[37] Thomas F. "From Tragedy to Triumph: Canadian Connections in the Management of Rhesus Hemolytic Disease of the Newborn." *Journal of Obstetrics and Gynaecology Canada* 41 (December 1, 2019). https://doi.org/10.1016/j.jogc.2019.08.038.

[38] Henry, King, director. *The Song of Bernadette.* Featuring Jennifer Jones. 20th Century Fox. 1943. 2 hr., 35 min.

my husband for help but couldn't utter a sound. He was standing four metres away, yet he had no idea what was happening to me. I was lucid but couldn't speak. I felt like a prisoner trapped in my own body. I looked down at my beautiful boy and began to pray. I said to the Virgin Mary, "Mary, as you were the mother to Jesus, I want to be a mother to my son. Please help me." In my mind I recited the Hail Mary and on the word Amen, my symptoms were resolved.

I thought the temporary incident was a result of just being overtired, so I didn't seek immediate medical attention. Unknowingly, I had experienced signs of a transient ischemic attack (TIA), otherwise known as a mini stroke. A few days after this clinical episode, I still felt unwell. I went to a walk-in clinic and was completely dismissed by the doctor. The following day I decided to go to the ER. The triage nurse assessing me was startled after observing how I had performed the task of standing eyes closed, arms extended, and palms facing upward. Instead of my arms remaining level, my right one slowly dropped to my side. She couldn't conceal her feelings of concern—they were evident in her eyes and knitted brows. Within seconds, a gurney was brought next to me, and I was whisked out of the room.

I spent a few nights in the hospital. Unconvinced of the doctor's conclusion and dissatisfied with the care that I had received, my husband drove me to the London Health Sciences Centre in London, Ontario, for a second opinion. Since it was the weekend and I wasn't deemed an urgent case, the physician felt I could wait for a follow-up appointment with an internist. My only thoughts were: *I don't have time to waste; I need to be around to take care of my family; I won't be deterred from finding answers sooner rather than later.* Unwilling to wait, we left for Beaumont Hospital in Royal

Oak, Michigan, after briefly stopping at our home to see our children. We were told the cost of cardiac testing and treatment would be "astronomical" and if I didn't receive certain tests in Canada within a week, I should return. My family physician then ordered an echocardiogram, which should have been performed while I was in the hospital. The results showed that I needed heart surgery—a right mini-thoracotomy—to repair an atrial septal defect. The cardiologist suspected that a postpartum clot had formed and passed through the hole in my heart and travelled to my brain. An inferoseptal aneurysm, the size of a golf ball, was unexpectedly found during the operation. The procedure started off dramatically and my life was in immediate danger, but once again, I survived.

Being a mother—with new responsibilities—changed me and my perspective on life. As a result, I became determined to be taken seriously when ill. I made an oath to myself that in the future, when necessary, I would search for answers until I was satisfied. I would not give up. Not having all the signs of a mini stroke recognized wasn't the first time I was improperly assessed but I was going to do my best to make it the last. I suffered from gallbladder attacks for six long years because I wasn't the typical textbook case—apparently this malady doesn't happen to a nineteen-year-old. I've often been misdiagnosed and grew tired of misconceptions based on my age and that I looked fine.

Over the years, I read medical journals and gained knowledge about my conditions, or ones that I believed I had. Being well-read on a disease, syndrome, or procedure, allows me to speak comfortably with a doctor. Even though I never disclose all that I've learned about a condition, many specialists have expressed appreciation that they are able to speak with an informed patient.

I've been asked if I studied medicine, told more than once that I should be written up in a medical journal, and recently during an ER visit, heartwarmingly called "a real warrior." The doctor, who said these impactful words, was ready to discharge me when I politely voiced that I couldn't leave the hospital without treatment. He calmly excused himself, indicating that he would be right back. When he re-entered the room, he explained, to my surprise, that he had left to read my medical files. He then sat down across from me, pulled his chair closer, and looked me in the eyes. He spoke with an authenticity that touched my soul so deeply that I later enjoyed repeating and reminding myself of his words. I was "a real warrior" and have "been through so much."

I have several conditions, which were diagnosed after I completed my memoir: Lynch Syndrome, a genetic mutation that predisposes me to certain types of cancer and requires regular follow-up; and Loeys-Dietz Syndrome (LDS), a rare genetic connective tissue disorder. I'm at risk of aneurysms, and arterial ruptures or dissections in any part of the entire arterial vascular tree—from the brain to the extremities—without forewarning. My geneticist in Toronto provided me with an emergency letter in case I develop certain symptoms and need to present to the ER. The note indicates that I should be triaged urgently. Since LDS is not a well-known condition, a 24/7-hour emergency number is provided should physicians have any questions regarding protocols to be followed during an emergency.

I have another undiagnosed condition. Six doctors have expressed concern and are baffled by my large left-sided supraclavicular lump. All scans were inconclusive. I researched my symptoms and prayed. Since no one was able to provide an explanation, I asked God to please reveal what was wrong with me in a dream. He answered me that night! But His response was not provided through a dream. Suddenly, I woke up, as if struck by a lightning bolt. A message was revealed to my heart: *Go on Facebook now!* I dismissed this strange prompting that jolted me out of sleep into a half-upright position. The message was repeated louder, and so emphatically, that it could not be ignored. The first post in my feed was from the Mayo Clinic, showing a side-view illustration of a woman with similar physical features as mine. Now, wide awake, at 4:00 a.m., I eagerly read the article that described Cushing's Syndrome.

I strongly suspect I have Cushing's Disease and have asked two doctors for their opinion. With certainty, they both said no. I disagree. I had a consultation with a doctor at a walk-in clinic for what I believed to be a rotator cuff tear. It was later confirmed that I did have a full thickness tear that required surgery. As the physician was about to exit the room, I felt an overwhelming urge to get her attention and express that I believe I have Cushing's Disease. I asked if she would order some bloodwork. She immediately looked at the back of my neck, felt this secondary lump, shrugged her shoulders as if to say, *sure, why not?* and quickly wrote up a lab requisition. With one key abnormal result, my family physician decided to investigate further and send me for another set of labs. The combination of results was suggestive of a brain tumour. I then had a sella turcica 3 Tesla MRI, which confirmed a pituitary microadenoma—a type of brain tumour that is associated with Cushing's. I wasn't the least bit surprised; I already knew it existed. The Lord had prepared me.

Currently, I'm being monitored by ten doctors for my various conditions, and have seen or spoken to nineteen doctors, specialists, and surgeons over the past few years. I also have other physical health problems. Feeling pain and experiencing frustration of not being heard or diagnosed properly are not new to me. But God, Mary, His angels, and saints, are with me every step of the way—ready to catch and raise me up when I fall.

My hope for you, my valued reader, is that you persevere through the challenges you may face, knowing that the extraordinary power of His divine love and mercy is at hand. You are never alone. Know that if you turn to Heaven, help is but a conversation away.

With love, Monique.

Bibliography

Baskett, Thomas F. "From Tragedy to Triumph: Canadian Connections in the Management of Rhesus Hemolytic Disease of the Newborn." *Journal of Obstetrics and Gynaecology Canada* 41 (December 1, 2019). https://doi.org/10.1016/j.jogc.2019.08.038.

Combes, Abbé André. *The Spirituality of St. Thérèse: An Introduction.* Third edition. New York: P.J. Kennedy & Sons, 1950.

Dahan, Olivier, director. *La Vie en Rose.* Featuring Marion Cotillard. Légende Films, TF1 International, Canal+, TPS Star. 2007. 2 hr., 20 min.

De Meester, Conrad. *With Empty Hands: The Message of St. Therese of Lisieux.* Translated by Mary Seymour. Washington, DC: ICS Publishing, 2002.

Descouvemont, Pierre, and Helmuth Nils Loose. *Therese and Lisieux.* Translated by Salvatore Sciurba and Louis Pambrun. Toronto: Novalis, 1996.

Gonzales, Loren. "St. Thérèse of Lisieux Seven Disguises In Which God Frequently Sends His Graces." Web log. *Overheard in the Sacristy* (blog), February 1, 2007. https://fiftysophomoricsummers.blogspot.com/search?q=Seven+Disguises.

Guernier, Pierre. "The Top Traditions of the French Christmas Tree." French Moments, February 7, 2022. https://frenchmoments.eu/french-christmas-tree-le-sapin-de-noel-en-france/.

Guernier, Pierre. "What Are the Christmas Tree Decorations in France?" French Moments, February 7, 2022. https://frenchmoments.eu/christmas-tree-decorations-in-france/.

Guernsey, Daniel P. *Adoration: Eucharistic Texts and Prayers throughout Church History.* San Francisco: Ignatius Press, 1999.

King, Henry, director. The Song of Bernadette. Featuring Jennifer Jones. 20th Century Fox. 1943. 2 hr., 35 min.

Kreb, Jean-Paul. "The beautiful and real story of the Christmas tree." Best of Upper Rhine, December 27, 2017. https://best-of-upper-rhine.com/selestat-alsace-real-history-of-the-christmas-tree/.

Liguori, Alphonsus. *Visits to The Most Holy Sacrament and The Blessed Virgin Mary.* Edited by R. A. Coffin. London: Burns & Lambert, 1855.

Lilles, Anthony, and Dan Burnes. "St. Thérèse's Act of Oblation to Merciful Love." St. Paul Centre for Biblical Theology. Accessed May 31, 2022. https://stpaulcenter.com/the-act-of-oblation-to-merciful-love/.

Lytton, Lytton Edward Bulwer. *The Parisians.* Estes and Lauriat, 1891.

Mallory, Thomas H. *The Man Behind the Mask: The Journey of an Orthopaedic Surgeon.* First edition. Columbia: University of Missouri Press, 2007.

Meconi, David Vincent, and Joseph Pearce. *The Confessions: St. Augustine of Hippo, With an Introduction and Contemporary Criticism.* First edition. San Francisco: Ignatius Press, 2012.

O'Riordan, Maureen, ed. "Eyewitness Accounts of the Exhumations of the Relics of St. Therese of Lisieux." October 19, 2010. Translated by Monique Pilon-Fraschetti for Saint Therese of Lisieux: A Gateway. From the Archives of the Carmel of Lisieux. http://www.thereseoflisieux.org/my-blog-about-st-therese/2010/10/19/relics-of-st-therese-of-lisieux-from-the-archives-of-the-lis.html.

Publisher of the NIV, Biblica. "Why Aren't Pronouns Referring to God Capitalized in Some Bibles." Bible Gateway. Biblica, May 9, 2019. https://support.biblegateway.com/hc/en-us/articles/228180527-Why-aren-t-pronouns-referring-to-God-capitalized-in-some-Bibles.

Soeur Thérèse Et Théophane Venard: Missions Étrangères, 350 ans d'histoire et d'aventure en Asie. Displayed at the Basilica of Lisieux.

Thérèse, of Lisieux (Saint). *Story of a Soul: The Autobiography of Saint Thérèse of Lisieux.* Third edition. Translated by John Clarke. Washington, DC: ICS Publications, 1996.

Thérèse, of Lisieux (Saint). *The Story of a Soul: The Autobiography of Saint Thérèse of Lisieux.* Edited by Mother Agnes of Jesus. Translated by Michael Day. Rockford, IL: TAN Books and Publishers, 1997.

Wilde, Oscar. "The Ballad of Reading Gaol by Oscar Wilde - Poems | Academy of American Poets." Poets.org. Academy of American Poets. Accessed May 16, 2022. https://libquotes.com/oscar-wilde/quote/lbx8n4r.